WHAT OTHERS ARE SAYING ABOUT
This Can't Be Happening to Me

"*This Can't Be Happening to Me* is a well written book recounting the life of a woman in crisis and the overwhelming needs she carries alone. The book is enlightening, moving and motivating. Thank you, Angela, for writing the story so many women have endured. May it equip us to bring hope, compassion and practical resources to young women throughout their crisis and remind us of our duty to do so." **Cindi Boston, CEO Pregnancy Care Center, MO**

"I have the joy of being a friend and pastor in Angela's life. Her powerful testimony will impact your heart. Her book is personal, very readable, refreshingly honest and will ultimately leave you with a desire to be more sensitive and available to those in need all around you."
Pastor Jeffrey S Slipp, Saddleback Church Anaheim

"I loved it, couldn't put it down. Thank you for sharing your story with such transparency. As I was reading it I was thinking of clients of ours that would benefit from reading it as well. It pains me to see that even though you chose life - the better thing - yet to be ousted and hurt. This really penetrated my heart. I know that the Christian community has grown and will continue to grow as stories like yours are told. Many blessings to you sister. I believe in my spirit God has plans for you greater than you can imagine. It is amazing how our God can take such sorrow and create such joy with it."
Rose Juarado, Modesto Pregancy Center, CA

"Finished your book last night. I do a lot of reading and I can honestly say, it's one of the best I have ever read. It's an easy read, meaning, it was like I was having a conversation with you. It drew me in...I didn't want to put it down! Some of your experiences, I have gone through also. So I, and most people, can relate to it in one way or another. A lot of people have went through the same experiences that you did, but you have a caring sense about you that makes you want to share it to help others. It has affected the way I think about life, my children and God." **Brian Woodcock, GA**

"Wow! This book is a "must read" for all. I am not a book reader but I read it in one day and couldn't put it down! It will affect your life in one way or another. It will show you how to handle situations whether you are in the position as a family member, church pastor or counselor. May everyone who reads this book learn, as I have, from the experiences that Angela went through, to help you know how to love & help others in their problems." **Sandy Gutierrez, IN**

This Can't Be Happening To Me

God is not surprised by your bad decisions...
God still has a plan

ANGELA STOUT

THIS CAN'T BE HAPPENING TO ME

ISBN 978-0-615-36619-7

Scripture quotations are taken from the Holy Bible, New Living
Translation (NLT), Copyright © 1996, 2004. Used by permission of
Tyndale House Publishers, Inc., Wheaton, Illinois 60189. All rights
reserved.

Composition/Song Title: MUCH TOO HIGH A PRICE
Writer Credits: GREG NELSON / PHILL MCHUGH
Copyright: © 1985 Greg Nelson Music (BMI) River Oaks Music
Company (BMI) (adm. by EMI CMG Publishing) / Careers BMG
Music (BMI). All rights reserved. Used by permission.

"Just Think" by Roy Lessin © 2010 DaySpring Cards. Used by
permission, all rights reserved. www.dayspring.com

AngelActOne Publishing and its angel design logo are trademarks of
AngelActOne Enterprises LLC and Angela Stout.

Printed in the United States of America
2010 – First Edition

DEDICATION

I want to, first of all, thank God for bringing me through those many rough times when I was alone. Without His presence in my life, who knows where I would be. Much thanks to my family, especially my children, who have endured through the good times and the bad over the years. I love you both more than you'll ever know.

I also want to thank the many people who helped direct me along the way as I began this journey to get my first book published. Thanks to Brett Miller for his encouragement and for leading me to Antonio L. Crawford, founder of the National Christian Writers Conference, who assisted me and directed me to some wonderful people that could help me accomplish this dream.

I appreciate the listening ears of friends and those who took time to read my manuscript before it came into print, as well as those who heard me speak—your tears showed the necessity of bringing this story to light. Your feedback and sincerity has been invaluable to me. Thank you, and with deepest gratitude I dedicate this book to all of you.

"This can't be happening to me."

These were exactly the words that leaped to my mind as I realized that I had set in motion the undoing of my own life.

I can only blame myself. I got stuck in my own Sodom and Gomorrah and it almost destroyed my life. I made poor choices and I had to live with the consequences and try to move on, and I may never realize a full redemption. Be that as it may, this is my story. Right or wrong. Good or bad. Beautiful or ugly. It is just the way it is.

When I originally began writing this book more than 15 years ago, I had a hidden agenda. I wanted to prove that my mistakes, my sins, were now vindicated because I was married and living a decent life. I wanted to show the pastors, the church congregation, the counselors, and everyone else that, even though I had screwed up, I had now arrived.

In their eyes, I was a royal mess-up: just out of college — Bible College, that is — pregnant out of wedlock, no father in sight, and no place to live. While I was pregnant, I was at the mercy of whoever would accept an outcast and, hence, I moved eight times in nine months. I was still trying to attend church, but I was ridiculed and looked down upon. Without constructive support, I spiraled downward.

So in my book, I wanted to "let all of them know" that God had worked everything out for the best and that I was blessed. But I have totally rewritten that first manuscript.

My hope for this book, the story of my mistakes and my struggles, is twofold: 1) that it will help people who have taken the wrong path to realize that they are capable of changing their behavior and circumstances rather than being destroyed by them, and that instead they can live a life of beauty and truth; and 2) that it will help people all over the world to understand how to support others in overcoming failure. It is easy to sit in judgment, but we are all human beings who make mistakes, who want to be loved and want to give love.

I would like to thank all those who helped me along my journey. Some of you I am still in touch with and some of you I have lost contact with. To all of you, thank you from the bottom of my heart for providing that "cup of cold water" when I really needed it. And thank you above all to God for working in my life and bringing me to where I am today.

To all of you reading this book, may you be blessed and changed by traveling with me on my tumultuous path…in this open book of mine.

~ With love, Angela

CONTENTS

Part I

CHAPTER ONE

Finding Out

"Oh, my God, this *can't* be happening to me." A sense of shock, fear and hopelessness gripped my heart as I learned that I was pregnant. Not that I was just pregnant, but that I was single and pregnant. And to add to my grief, I had spent the past four years in Bible College! I had graduated in May with my class, walking the line for the Associate of Arts in Music, and here I was in August finishing my last few weeks of classes to receive the Bachelor of Arts in Bible when I found out that I was pregnant. As a requirement for my Bachelor's degree, I was also doing an internship at a local church. Every Sunday morning, I sat on the platform with the other pastors on staff in front of the congregation and participated throughout the week in the church office administratively. I was also known as a singer in various churches throughout the Midwest and had even recorded a solo album at age 19. In other words, I was standing at the threshold of possibly a great ministry opportunity and I blew it.

All I truly desired was to minister about God and his wonderful plan of salvation, deliverance and healing and I sold it for one moment—one bit of time—that would change the course of my life forever. Just like Esau selling his birthright to satisfy one temporary fix of hunger, I would learn soon enough the bitterness of my mistake and I would experience many difficult years from the domino effect of my wrong decisions.

Getting to the point of "finding out" was probably the slowest, grueling month I had ever experienced. I never thought that meeting Nick during that summer would take my life down such a long, dark path. Close to the time we met, I had moved into an apartment with Debbie, a Seminary student. Nick was 28 and I was 22. He had just come to Bible College to begin his study to minister as a chaplain in the Armed Forces. He had also been in the Navy for several years, serving both active and reserve. Although he chose to attend a charismatic denominational college, he had a strong Catholic background and regularly attended mass. I was uncomfortable with this situation, but I was a bit relieved when he came to the church where I was interning. He didn't quite get the lifting up of hands to worship God, but he was respectful and earned the approval of a few of my church friends. After that visit, I was encouraged to go with him to mass but we never did go together.

I guess what kept me being friends with Nick, even though I was concerned about the religious differences, was that he initially seemed respectful and caring. I think the defining moment for me was when I was being attacked verbally by a jealous girl in the cafeteria and he immediately came to my rescue. I always appreciated a man who could stand up for himself and protect others at the same time. It was the sense of security and protectiveness that drew me in.

Nick and I had dated a couple of times and my interest in him cautiously grew. On the 4th of July, we decided to have a picnic and pool party at my apartment complex. We invited a few friends but most of my friends were out of town, including my roommate. Nick brought a friend with him and we enjoyed swimming and tanning for a good portion of the afternoon until we were hungry enough to get started on the grill. We gathered our belongings and headed to the apartment. We barely got started firing up the grill when his friend said he had to leave but would be back later to eat with us. So Nick and I were left to finish setting up and preparing the meal. After about an hour, the food was ready and his friend still had not returned, so we decided to eat without him and leave him a plate for when he returned.

We had a good dinner and an interesting conversation. Nick mentioned a long live-in relationship he had had, but was unwilling to talk much about the situation. Though I tried to ask more questions, he dismissed them. The conversation moved on to religion—how we were raised and our beliefs. He had been raised Catholic and still attended mass, and he again invited me to go with him. His attending the Bible College seemed like a contradiction to his own beliefs and was definitely opposed to the way I was raised. When he spoke of being a chaplain, I really couldn't see him doing that, nor could I see how my life would fit with that type of ministry. I was always contemplating the future with the thought of marrying someone and how ministry would fit with marriage. But apparently this day, I wasn't focused on that; I somehow ignored all the red flags. After finishing dinner, there was still no sign of his friend, and we continued our conversation in the

4

living room. Up to that point, I had been calm, with a "matter of fact" attitude as I was getting to know him, but then our eyes met, which was something I had tried to avoid. His deep brown eyes drew me in and he pulled my hair aside and kissed me. I nervously tried to continue the conversation, focusing on myself this time and telling him what God had been doing in my life and what I was hoping to do. I even shared an important message that had been given to me but he seemed aloof and disinterested. I knew he wasn't listening to a word I had to say, but I overlooked all the bright red flags that God gave me.

I was drawn to him in such a powerful way that when he kissed me again I didn't even attempt to end it. His friend finally came back and knocked on the door but he encouraged me not to answer it. Then, as they say, one thing led to another. And all the while this was going on, I heard the voice telling me over and over to stop. "Stop! You've got to stop." I ignored that voice—the voice of the Holy Spirit. I rejected the One who knows what is best for me and listened instead to the father of lies. Immediately, I was overcome with fear and guilt. I rushed to the bathroom, hoping to flush out any possibility of my becoming pregnant. I told Nick I was scared and that this was so close after my period. He gave me some advice which I took, thinking he was a man that had gotten around and knew the ropes. He told me to douche it out. I believe that spurred it on! No matter what I did, I sensed I was in trouble. Not long after that, Nick left and I prayed, "God please forgive me and please don't let me be pregnant! I'll never do that again!"

The next day, I decided that I would confide in a friend and I went to Krystn's house. Krystn was the wife of Scott, who was a student at the college. I was afraid to tell her what had happened, but I needed to confide in and be accountable to someone so that this would not happen again. Krystn welcomed me in and I nervously told her what I had done. She asked me if I had asked forgiveness from God and I told her I had, but I felt like I wanted to ask his forgiveness again with her. We prayed together. One questioned remained as I looked up at Krystn and asked timidly, "What if I'm pregnant?" Krystn reassured me and told me not to worry because it was highly unlikely that I was pregnant. Still, I knew I would not be satisfied until I knew for sure. And so the wait began, and it seemed as if every minute of every day was being counted out loud in my head.

During this time, I moved out of the apartment

and back into the hot dorm. The dorm was in an old building with no air conditioning, so the only way to get relief from the hot July heat was by putting a fan in the window. As I settled in, I tried to relieve the pressure of the "what if" question by burying myself in my studies and focusing on finishing my Bachelor's degree over the next couple of weeks. But then the last week came. Those days seemed especially lonely. Every morning I woke up with new anxiety as I walked down the corridor with the creaky floors beneath my feet to the hallway showers and restrooms, hoping for "that time of the month." Day after day, it didn't come. Once again I went to Krystn in near panic.

"Angela, don't get too worried and uptight about it or you could actually slow the arrival of your period," she said in a comforting tone. She encouraged me to wait a few more days and then if nothing happened we would go to the nearest Crisis Pregnancy Center. She even called them and asked them questions as to how long I needed to wait and what I needed to do.

I headed back to classes with a heavy mind and heart. The classes went by in a kind of fog; I was so weighted down by my anxiety. I remember one day when a faculty member approached me as I was walking out of the dorm. With concern in her eyes and voice she asked, "Are you doing all right? I have had a burden in my heart to pray for you." I told her that something could be really bad and to please keep praying for me. She said she would continue praying and reminded me that God was with me and that everything was going to be all right. As I walked away, I felt the worst was about to happen, because you normally don't tell a person that everything's going to be all right when all is well. Either the Lord was preparing me for the worst scenario or I was thinking too much.

As for Nick, he was easy going. He encouraged me to go on a 2 or 3-mile jog around the area with him, which I did to prove my athletic abilities. When the fair came to the city, we went together, but things between us seemed aloof. We passed by a pro-life booth and a part of me wanted to stop, but I was too afraid. As we came upon the exciting array of rides, he urged me to go on the swirling Spider. I turned to him, "What if I'm pregnant?" He flippantly retorted, "It'll be all right! Come on!" I got in line with him, wondering if he cared or not if I was pregnant and that I could lose the baby.

That same week back at the dorm, I bumped into Dan as I was heading back up to my room.

Dan was an older cousin of a Bible student there, and occasionally he would come to visit. I had first met him when they both visited the church I attended. A few weeks later I ran into them at the cafeteria and Dan had both of his elementary-age children with him. He had been going through his own struggles, having been separated for three-and-a-half years. Though he was a nice guy, I was not interested in anything other than friendship. Plus, having been raised in a strict religious environment, I had my own standards concerning divorced people: I strongly believed that you should never date or marry a divorced person. But here he was, at a time when I was struggling, asking me how everything was going. All I could tell him was that I was having a hard time and things weren't going too well. He smiled and with compassion said to let him know if there was anything he could do to help. We shared some small talk and then went our separate ways.

By now, enough time had gone by for me to get a pregnancy test. Day after day of going to the shower room down that long dark hallway had turned up no sign of what I was hoping for. What I thought were symptoms of my period approaching were possibly symptoms of what I had been dreading. Krystn told me that I was to take a morning urine sample into the Crisis Pregnancy Center for testing. The preparations were made, and for support, Krystn picked me up at the campus to take me there. She tried her best to keep me cool and calm. Afraid of being seen and not wanting to divulge my name, I asked Krystn if she would take the sample in to be tested. We ended up parking in a lot next to the center, which, ironically, was the parking lot for the abortion clinic. Reacting in fear and guilt, I slid way down in my seat so that no one could see me while she went in for the testing. Krystn explained the situation to the ladies in the office in hopes that they would give the test without making me come in — something the center does not normally do. They continued on with the testing, while emphasizing to Krystn that if it turned out positive they would like to see me. Krystn assured them that I was not abortion minded and that she would have me come in if the test was positive.

In the meantime, I was hiding out in her car, thinking: "This isn't such a great place to park either. What's taking Krystn so long? What's going on in there? I must be pregnant or she wouldn't be taking so long. Oh, God, please don't let me be pregnant!" As my thoughts raced, cries and pleas came from my heart like a flood that I thought would drown me. Then she came to the door....

She got in the car, closed the door, and without any words started the car.

"So, Krystn, what happened, am I...?"

Krystn turned to me with pamphlets in her hand. "Angela, you are pregnant and you will have to start taking special care of yourself...."

The rest of what she was saying became a blur in my head. Tears welled up in my eyes, but I was too numb to really cry. The overwhelming sense of shock, disbelief, and fear that came over me was indescribable. "Oh my God, this can't be happening to me. This just can't be happening to me. Oh my God, what am I going to do?" My life felt like it had been crushed flat, and that all hope had been sucked out of me.

After the drive back to the dorm, Krystn walked with me to the class hall and pulled her husband, Scott, out of class to give him the news. Nick happened to be in that class and saw the three of us in a serious discussion outside the room. Scott looked intently at my distraught face and softly confirmed their love and support for me. "We're going to be praying for you. Everything's going to work out. You'll be just fine."

Scott headed back into the class and Krystn had to take care of other matters. So here I was – alone – still in shock and confusion. Nick had figured out what the three of us were talking about, but in the cafeteria he wanted to hear it for himself. "Well, are you?" he asked.

"Yes…yes, I'm pregnant," I floundered. He smiled, put his arm around me, and led me out of the cafeteria in a cocky sort of way.

Once outside, he dropped his arm and shoved his hands in his pockets like he had just accomplished something he had worked for. He seemed uncannily pleased. I tried to follow his strange lightheartedness by saying that if it was a girl, she would be very beautiful. He added, "And if it's a boy, he'll be suave and debonair like me." Then we parted to go to our own classes, and I was unsure of what any of this meant or what kind of support I might see from him.

Prior to this, he hadn't been part of the conversations regarding the possibility of me being pregnant. In fact, he had given me very little attention at all after meeting with me at the apartment. He had gone off and done what he felt like doing, while I was waiting to find out. Strangely, when he found out that I was pregnant, he seemed to be happy with himself. However, he offered me no support of any kind that day and I sensed that he wouldn't be offering me support in the future.

The day dragged on with the professor's words muffled in my brain. I knew that I would soon enough have to tell others: Dad, Mom, the pastor at the church where I was interning, and maybe a school counselor. Maybe I would wait a long time to tell my parents. Or maybe I would just stay here — a ten hour drive from where they were — and wait until after the baby was born and after I had given the baby up for adoption. I would just have to make sure they didn't come to see me and I would have to give them a good reason as to why I wasn't coming home. Maybe I would do the unthinkable. No, *I couldn't do that!* I just need some sleep. Maybe things would be different in the morning. Maybe I would wake up only to find that all this had been a big bad dream!

I was in bed by 9:00 pm physically and mentally exhausted. Sleep wouldn't bless me, though — I tossed and turned. How was I going to share this with everyone? Would I still receive my bachelor's degree? What would my future be like now? Tears trickled down my face as I reached out for a different realty – something other than this. I couldn't take it anymore. I needed someone to help me NOW! I needed to relieve the burden that I was carrying, yet I was afraid of the response I would get. Would they be angry with me? Would they be harsh with me? Would they be forgiving? I began fumbling for a quarter to use for the pay phone. It was midnight. Should I call Dad? What were they going to say? I had to get it over with. I had to tell them.

I made my way down the same dark corridor where I had built up so much anxiety over the past month. "God help me. Don't let them be too angry with me." The phone booth was situated at the corner of two hallways and the only form of privacy was a curtain that could be pulled shut. Conversations could still be heard by anyone close enough and who might be in the booth could possibly be guessed by the person's legs and shoes. I huddled myself as close to the back corner of the booth as possible and my heart began pounding. "Jesus, help me," I whispered. My hands began to shake as I dropped in the quarter and dialed the number.

As the phone rang, my breath became shallow and I was tempted to hang up the phone. But then he answered. "Dad," I stammered, my voice quivering. "I've got something to tell you. I've done something terrible."

Dad's sleepy voice immediately came alive. "Now what?" he questioned. His response made me wonder what else he thought I had done wrong. I thought I had always tried to do things right to make them proud of me. Without much time to think and no way of turning back now, the words fell from my lips: "Dad, I'm pregnant."

In instant anger he exclaimed, "You stupid! Of all the stupid things…"

"Dad, I don't need to be hearing that right now," I blurted. "What do you want me to do—get an abortion?"

He responded no, that it would only make things worse. He suggested I come back home.

"But I have school—only have two weeks left."

"What good is it going to do you now?"Dad snapped.

"I don't know. But I am going to stay and finish." Those words made me wonder why I should stay, or if it would be worth it to finish a Bible degree now anyway. Yet I felt determined to finish it after all my years of hard work.

Dad told me he would have to talk to me later and that they would need some time to think about things. I wanted to know how long and he said, "A few days." We both hung up. The only relief was that the burden of hiding my secret was now lifted, but the weight of loneliness and despair felt worse.

That week I felt deserted. I felt deserted not only from my earthly father but also from my heavenly Father. The loneliness became a dull, ceaseless pain in my heart. Then my sister called.

"Well, I heard…" She wanted to know all the details. Who was he? How long had I been seeing this guy? The one thing she couldn't swallow was that my pregnancy happened after only one encounter. "Oh, come on. You mean to tell me you only did it one time and you're pregnant?" she asked in disbelief as if I was lying.

"Yes, it only happened once," I confirmed sadly. I knew it would be hard for her to believe, because she and her husband had been trying to have another baby and were using fertility drugs, just as they had the first time they conceived. I felt bad. I wished it was her instead of me. It *should* have been her instead of me. Here I was in a position I didn't want to be in, yet my sister so desperately wanted to be pregnant. After we hung up, I breathed a prayer to God, "Please let my sister get pregnant." I was afraid that if she didn't get pregnant that she would become bitter toward me. And perhaps God heard my prayer because my sister did get pregnant only two weeks later!

Not only did this affect my sister; it also affected one of my brothers, who was in the Air Force and stationed overseas with his wife. Bitter feelings poured out through a letter that my brother sent to my parents, which he later shared with me, about how certain members of the family treated them when his then girlfriend, now wife, became pregnant out of wedlock. Then I heard from my older brother and his wife that they were willing to adopt my baby. With all the tense emotions, an already confusing situation was getting worse.

At the end of that very long week, my dad finally called. My first concern was what Mom thought. "She cried," he answered. Our discussion turned to the father of the baby and if we were going to get married. I didn't have much of an answer for him, since there wasn't much of anything to say about Nick and me. When Nick and I spoke, there was no hint of marriage, and with his attitude I wasn't sure if I wanted to be with someone like him anyway. Scott had tried to speak with Nick about staying here and supporting me, but Scott honestly didn't see much hope for that.

Scott was right. Nick finished off the summer quarter and went back to his small hometown in

Missouri, rarely to be heard from again, and at no time did he offer any kind of financial support. I knew that I would not be able to count on Nick and that I had to move forward with what was right for me and the baby.

Dad suggested once again that I come home. I couldn't even think about that possibility. Once you've lived away from home for four years, it's hard to go back. Plus I couldn't handle the scorn and ridicule I was sure to get from the church back home. If there was anything I was insistent on was that I would not go back home. I just couldn't do that.

My pregnancy was kept quiet so that I could finish my degree. I did tell a professor who was also a college counselor, and I told the President of the college. Other than those two staff members, Nick, my friends Scott and Krystn, and my close family members, no one else knew. Even with the groundwork laid for me to finish the school year, I still felt the need to tell one more person – my pastor – but I was afraid to tell him. His church was where I had become a member while attending college and where I was doing my internship. I would have to wait to tell him at the office the following week.

Then it was Sunday morning. I was standing

on the platform as an intern, fully overwhelmed. I knew I was forgiven and I was trusting in God's forgiveness, yet I felt guilty, ashamed and scared. The pastor preached a message of healing to those who were overcome by sin and needed a way out. I wanted to burst. I couldn't wait for the service to be over with. I had to talk to the pastor today! Certainly after *that* message I would find him to be caring and compassionate. After what seemed like an unusually long altar time, I went to the pastor and asked if I could speak with him in private. We went to his spacious office and he assumed the pastoral position behind his desk with his hands folded in front of him. With his head cocked to the side and a slight smile on his face, he asked me what he could help me with. While wringing my hands with wadded tissues and tears streaming down my face, I explained the whole story and my progress up to that moment.

His first response was to advise me to move to Washington to attend his brother's church where "they knew how to handle situations like these." After a few moments, he calmly offered the church's support and said a prayer with me. That was it. It seemed like an all too abrupt end to a serious meeting. No discussion of counseling sessions, or what my plans were, or how I was doing, or what financial support I had, or where I would live when I left the dorm in a few weeks. Nothing. After the prayer, he got up from his seat, opened the office door, and gave a few more encouraging words as I was escorted out of the room. He *seemed* okay but something inside of me said that things were not okay.

I went back to the dorm with the same empty feelings – as if I had absolutely no one. Little did I know that this was just the beginning of a long, painful process of turmoil in my heart and soul. The consequences of my past decisions and more wrong decisions that I would make in the future were going to cause me years of pain and regrets.

CHAPTER TWO
Finding a Home

During the first two weeks after I found out I was pregnant, it was announced that I and the other students had to move to a different dorm so that remodeling work could begin in the old dorm where we had been staying. I didn't look forward to the move, particularly because I had to have a roommate for the last month there. I knew that I would have to be very cautious so my roommate wouldn't become suspicious. But hiding "the problem" would be much easier than hiding how I felt about the room temperature on any given day.

We shared a thermostat with an adjoining room, and though three of the four girls felt the temperature was fine, I found it cold. When I decided to confront one of the other girls about how cold it was and take it upon myself to turn it up, we got into a little spat. As I walked away with all the anger and hurt from everything else going on in my life, I muttered a condescending word. She came rushing up to me… "What did you say?" I knew I was wrong but I didn't offer an apology. What I really wanted to tell her was how messed up my life had become and that what I said was just a reflection of the emotions penned up inside of me. But right now wasn't the time. I had to finish the course and receive the other degree I had worked so hard on.

By late afternoon, I received a warning from the hall counselor that if it ever happened again that I could be expelled. She had talked with the dean of students and that was where I needed to be heading to. I was nervous but knew I couldn't reveal the source of my anguish at this time. After a brief conversation with the dean, we decided that an apology to the offended girl was best. I went immediately and took care of the matter. I apologized also to the hall counselor and told her that it would never happen again. She asked if there was anything I'd like to talk about. With tears in my eyes and my heart ready to break, I said, "I've just got a lot of things going on in my life right now—pretty bad, pretty bad." My head and my eyes lowered to the ground. "But I just can't talk about it right now." With sympathy, she said she hoped that I had someone to confide in and that if I ever wanted to, I could talk with her. But I knew I would never be able to open up to her because I didn't trust her. Nor could I entrust the details of my circumstance to anyone until my classes were completed.

I was able to hold on and finish my Bachelor's degree…but for what? I didn't know why I was so determined to get something I'd probably never be able to use. Who was I trying to fool? What was I proving by getting a Bible degree in the condition I was in? The pastor no doubt wanted me to just pass my internship and get out of there. All I had worked for now seemed to be for nothing. My only hope – the hope that kept me going for that degree was the slight possibility that I would be able to use it *someday*.

Right on the heels of all this drama, it was almost time to get out of the dorm to prepare for the fall semester. In those last two weeks, I managed to find a good doctor. An acquaintance of mine, Kelly, who was the mother of a child that attended the day care I was working at, recommended a young gynecologist that was very well liked. Since he was accepting new patients, I was able to set up an appointment.

In the meantime, I made a three-hour trip, with my friend, Rachel, to visit a home for unwed mothers who had chosen to place their babies up for adoption. The adoption agency was three hours away and my hesitation grew as we drove there. Rachel assured me that this trip was to see if this could possibly be an option for me and to confirm in my heart whether I wanted to raise this child or give the child up for adoption. The home for un-wed mothers was Christian-owned and the babies were placed with caring Christian families. As Rachel and I were taken on a tour of the place, I tried to imagine myself living there and giving my child away at birth. I couldn't see it. How could I stay in this home for the next eight months and give my baby up to some other family?

I went in to speak with one of the counselors. She explained all the details of daily schedules, obtaining the release of the biological father's rights, how they would cover the prenatal care, and the selection of the adoptive family. She asked questions about me and about the father. After our discussion, she had the papers readily available for me to sign if I was ready to make that decision. As she spoke about it, my thoughts became clouded. Yet the more we talked, the more I felt that I couldn't go through with it. Rachel thought it was a good place to go, but she knew that the decision was mine to make and that giving up my own child would be hard for me to do. We made the trip back home still not knowing what direction I would be heading.

Not long after our trip, I had my first appointment with the gynecologist. Dr. Otto seemed to be a caring doctor and offered a listening ear. I knew right away that I wanted him for my doctor throughout my pregnancy. He asked if I wanted a pregnancy test to confirm that I was pregnant and I chose to have a second test, hoping that maybe all along this was just a fluke. But when the doctor came back in the room with the results, I was still pregnant. Dr. Otto and I seemed to have personalities that could feed off the humorous and cynical side of situations. So we made light of what we already knew. I was able to share with him my mixed up situation and he offered up the possibility of adoption with a family that he knew was looking to adopt. But I told him I didn't think I could do that. He reassured me and told me that if I changed my mind I should let him know. His support and his ease in speaking with me gave me a sense of calmness that I hadn't experienced in a while. For once, I knew everything would be okay and I was completely satisfied with my new doctor.

But a problem occurred when the financial advisor asked how I was going to pay for the medical services. I told them that my father's insurance would cover most of it and the rest my father would take care of. They were satisfied with that until I found out that my father's insurance would only cover me if I was living at home. With no desire to return home in my condition, I soon learned that my only other option was to become a recipient of Medicaid and food stamps. At that time, most doctors were not thrilled about taking on Medicaid patients due to the difficulty of receiving payments in a timely manner. So on my next visit to Dr. Otto, I had to break the news to him. I told him my situation and pleaded with him to take me as his patient. Although he wasn't crazy about the idea, he agreed to take me on and I was tremendously thankful. He encouraged me and assured me that everything would be all right. I then left his office with another daunting task to prepare for…another move.

A middle-aged couple from the church came to my rescue and decided to help me in my distress. They saw how I was being ignored and pushed aside, and they decided to help me and give me a little hope. They found an apartment for me and they co-signed and took care of one month's rent. I moved in right away which was a fairly easy task since I didn't own much. Outside of personal items and clothing, I had only a phone, a stereo, and an old foam mattress that I laid on the floor for my bed. The family also brought me a few kitchen items, but my apartment was bare of any furniture whatsoever.

With a new apartment and mounting expenses, I began focusing on my job search. Somehow I landed a job in the hospital as an emergency room secretary. I'll never quite understand how I landed that job. At that time I had only basic computer skills and no experience whatsoever with medical terminology. After two weeks, the stress of the fast-paced job, my lack of experience, and my personal troubles began to show. My supervisor and I both agreed that the job was way over my head, so I gave my notice and was gone in two weeks.

Once again, loneliness and fear crept into my soul as I knew I had no more money coming in, that the father of my child was not supporting me in any way, and that the people who helped me get into this apartment were not able to make my rent payments while I looked for another job. On top of this, I had been virtually deserted both spiritually and emotionally by my own pastor and church.

One Sunday evening, I sat on the floor of my empty apartment as loneliness and despair enveloped me like a cloud. As usual, I turned to Christian music to console me. There was a particular song that I hoped to hear. While I sat there listening to the other music playing, I was desperately trying to remember the title of the song that was in my heart. After several minutes, I picked up the phone and called the station. "Could you play 'Much Too High A Price' by Larnelle Harris?" I asked brokenly. They said they'd try to find it.

Finally, the song came on. I sat there Indian style on the bare floor with my hands cupped over my faced and began sobbing as the music played.

Your love endured the cross
Despising all the shame,
That afternoon when midnight fell,
Your suffering cleared my name.
And that sin swept hill became the open door to paradise,
Because you paid so high a price.

You paid much too high a price for me,
Your tears, your blood, the pain
To have my soul just stirred at times,

Yet never truly changed.
You deserve a fiery love
That won't ignore your sacrifice,
Because you paid much too high a price.

Your grace inspires my heart
To rise above the sin
And all the earthly vanities
That seek to draw me in.
I want to tell this jaded world of love
That truly saved my life,
A love that paid so high a price.

There is a fountain filled with blood
Drawn from Emmanuel's veins.
And sinner's plunge beneath that flood
Lose all their guilty stains.

You deserve a fiery love that won't
ignore your sacrifice
Because You paid much too high a price.[1]

1 Composition/Song Title: MUCH TOO HIGH A PRICE. Writer Credits: GREG NELSON/PHILL MCHUGH. Copyright: ©1985 Greg Nelson Music (BMI) River Oaks Music Company (BMI) (adm. by EMI CMG Publishing) / Careers BMG Music (BMI). All rights reserved. Used by permission.

My heart was heavy. I curled up on the hard floor and cried. There seemed to be nothing that could soothe my aching soul. I wanted to believe that God still loved me, that He forgave me, and that somehow He would use me again someday. I needed someone to put their arms around me and hold me. I needed someone to tell me that they loved me and assure me that everything would be okay. But there was no one.

I wanted someone to see my heart. If they could only see it, they'd know that I really did love the Lord and I only wanted to serve Him. I had made such a mess of my life and now I begged God, over and over, to forgive me. Since others were not forgiving me and were deserting me, would God respond to me in the same way? Would He leave me too? I couldn't forgive myself either for making such a mess of my life.

To me, there did not seem to be any kind of hope…although I do remember a discussion I had with another girl while we were lounging by the poolside. "Maybe God will just bring someone into my life that will not care if I'm pregnant and will become the father of my child," I mused, acknowledging that it was just a crazy dream. "You know, Angela, it can really happen," she replied. God just might do that for you. I know someone in a similar situation like yours and…" off she went with the story. I wanted to believe in some sort of fairy tale ending, but the reality of life struck a sad chord in my heart.

By now, I was not only hopping churches; I was hopping addresses. I hated to, but I had to tell the apartment manager that I needed to get out of the lease agreement because I had lost my job and couldn't make the monthly payments. He grudgingly released me, commenting: "I should make those who co-signed for you pay. They are legally responsible." But he let me go and with great gratitude and appreciation, I thanked him. The only requirement was that I get myself out of there as quickly as possible. I had been there less than a month and now I was finding myself moving my meager possessions again. But where to this time?

With no time to look, I imposed myself upon some friends that had a new baby and who attended the church I had left because of the rejection I was feeling from the Pastor and his wife. I knew I couldn't stay there long – just a few days until I could find a place to go.

I continually checked with the Crisis Pregnancy Center, begging for help in finding a place to live.

Finally, a widowed sixty-something-year-old woman in the countryside decided to put me up until my baby was born. Arriving at her house, via a long driveway that led up to the barn-shaped house, I noticed how pretty her huge front yard was. I was relieved and excited at the sight; I hadn't known what kind of home I would be going to. Ruby was a kind, soft-spoken woman who made wonderful home cooked meals that would make anyone feel at home. Her home was as impressive as the yard, with many spacious rooms, and large windows with picturesque views of beautiful trees and landscaping. After touring the living area, she led the way to my room upstairs.

I nervously made chit-chat with her as she showed me my room. The room was large enough to make the queen-sized bed look small and the closet was more than I needed for my meager belongings. I knew instantly that I would feel comfortable here. She continued leading me through the house and then finished the tour back downstairs in the kitchen. Ruby had prepared a snack and we sat down. The windows in the dining area were expansive and gave one the feeling of being outdoors. Ruby told me that the deer would sometimes come up close to the windows to feed. We finished our snack and she took me to see the back yard. The yard was a portion of the two acres her house sat on and provided a private hideaway with large trees lining the boundaries of the two-acre property. The landscaping featured a small bridge, and best of all, a porch with a swing. I felt a sense of relief when I saw the swing. Swings were a big part of my childhood, and I would spend a lot of time swinging my problems away or dreaming up a beautiful future for my life. I knew right away that the swing would be a place for me to sort out the difficulties I was going through in my life. By this time, I was already beginning to feel at home.

I went with Ruby to her church, but even though it seemed nice, I didn't feel that was where I was supposed to be. But then, did I have a right to feel like I belonged anywhere with what I had done? Though I had asked forgiveness from God, I hadn't even begun to forgive myself. I needed to hear the family of God tell me that they forgave me. I wanted to find a church that would forgive me and support me through this pregnancy and counsel me in the path I should follow.

I continued my search. After visiting one particular church a few times, I made an appointment with the pastor and his wife to share my situation with them and get an idea of how I might be treated there. Needless to say, I felt more like an extra baggage to their small church than a welcomed family member. The pastor's response to my story came in a form of a nonchalant question tinged with sarcasm. "Well, what do you want us to do for you?" I thought to myself, 'Why do I have to answer that question? He should know what I want from them. What does anyone want to hear in my situation?' I didn't want them to *do* anything for me. It was what I needed to hear that was important to me and the tone in his voice was miles away from the compassion that I craved. I was looking for a compassionate pastor and a loving church to say, "We forgive you. We love you and there is no condemnation here. We will be here for you."

His attitude made me stumble for words. I felt empty and belittled as I tried to say that I just needed their support. The session wrapped up quickly with the pastor letting me know that if that was all I wanted, they could do that for me, but his tone and attitude did not match his words. I knew it; my spirit knew it; I left just as empty as when I had come. I never went back there, nor did I ever get a call from that pastor or anyone else in that church asking how I was or why I hadn't come back.

No one from any of the churches I had visited

called to say they missed me or to ask how I was doing. I mused over how churches are supposed to be examples of God. "If these churches are supposed to be an extension of Christ, then what did God think of me?" I asked myself. Maybe God had forgiven me – but then again maybe not. I knew I had asked Him to forgive me, but maybe He was going to hold this over my head.

One afternoon I sat down with Ruby in the living room and talked about my experiences with the churches. I told her that, oddly enough, I desired to go back to my home church – the one church that discarded me as a problem and wanted to ship me off to Washington. I couldn't explain it. The last time I had visited was a few weeks before when a group from another church I had attended went there to do a kid's crusade. The service was enjoyable, and though a couple of people were friendly to me, the atmosphere was still uneasy. And I felt that if someone was nice to me, it might just be the result of them not knowing that I was pregnant. That had been the case when I ran into Dan again with his cousin Tim. They asked me if I was going to the church skate night. I mumbled an excuse and graciously declined. Ruby patiently listened to me talk. Her only advice was that maybe I should try again. "After all, what's the worst thing that could happen?" she asked. The worst thing that could happen was that they could publicly humiliate me and kick me out, but I didn't really think that would happen, so I decided to go back that night and see if anything had changed.

Nervous, I walked in alone. I was afraid that people would stare at me and begin whispering. I searched desperately for someone to sit with, someone who would be a little compassionate. My anxiety welled up as service time was getting closer. Frantically, I looked across the congregation, and finally my eyes landed on Marshal and Jan – the couple that I had stayed with for a couple of days. They didn't seem ashamed of me and even had me sit with them. As the singing began, I noticed several people glancing at me, not only from those in their seats but also from those on the platform. I felt completely uncomfortable and I tried to calm down by focusing on the songs. I closed my eyes and asked God to help me as I made an attempt to worship Him.

The service sped by and all I could really remember was my feelings of inadequacy, rejection, and loneliness. I was glad it was over. The pastor and his wife made no attempt to greet me nor did anyone else on staff. Tim and his cousin Dan were, once again, friendly and cordial; presumably they didn't know what was going on with me. They asked if I was doing anything and if I wanted to go get some pizza with them. "Sure," I said hesitantly. We hopped in Tim's car and headed to the pizza place.

The conversation warmed up over the scrumptious pepperoni pizza and I even had a few laughs. But I was uneasy. If they knew, would they be like the rest and talk about me behind my back? If they didn't know yet, would they desert me like everyone else when they found out? On the way back to the church, I decided that when Tim dropped Dan and me off at our own cars, I would tell Dan and see what his reaction was. I could handle rejection from one person but not from two. At least if I told Dan, he could tell Tim and they could silently go away and not deal with me anymore, if that's what they decided. I knew there was an excellent chance that they would never talk to me again, but I also knew that it was not fair for them to find out through someone else or, even worse, for someone to think that either one of them had anything to do with my pregnancy. This way gave them an "easy out." Just because my reputation was ruined, I didn't need to ruin someone else's through the ignorance of others.

We pulled up into the nearly empty church parking lot and Dan and I said our goodbyes to Tim. As Dan and I began walking to our cars, he started to tell me his situation. He had been separated from his wife for over three years and had made some attempts to get back together, but to no avail. I couldn't imagine being separated from someone that long and not moving on with my life, but I didn't question him further. I was so anxious to tell him about my own situation that I wasted no time.

The autumn night was chilly, so we got into his car as I began to spill out my story. The only way I knew how to begin was by preceding my confession with a warning. "Now this is really bad. It's not good what I've done, but I have asked forgiveness and I'm trying to go on with my life. If you and Tim don't want to be around me after I tell you this, I'll understand, okay?"

For some reason he didn't appear too concerned. How bad could it be, after all? This was a girl he had seen sing on the church platform and sit amongst the pastors on staff. With the hope that there might be a little support there, I carefully told my story while watching for his response. I was so hungry for attention. I wanted someone…anyone…to love me, to forgive me, to accept me, to help me in some way.

If he didn't accept me, who would?

There. The truth was out. I am three months pregnant. I was ready for the abrupt cold shoulder and a quick push out of the car, but I got neither. He had a look of compassion as he asked a question that touched me deeply. "Can I give you a hug?" Though somewhat numb from the question, I nodded my head. He gave me a hug. In that moment, I thought, "Why couldn't anyone else from the churches I visited have done that?" This is all that I had been longing for… forgiveness, acceptance, love and a hug. And here I was exchanging phone numbers with a man that was still legally married, and even if he was divorced, I would still have issues with him. He had two children, and I was in no way ready to be a mom myself, let alone take care of someone else's children. But this is someone who gave me what I needed in the moment. As he handed me his phone number, he told me to call if I needed anyone to talk to.

Wow! When the church doesn't step in, someone will step in. When someone makes a terrible mistake it is not the time for the church to shrink back and "let them handle their own problems." Of course I called Dan. Who else should I call? I was considered a reprobate, an outcast, a sinner "caught in the act." No one cared and I felt so desperate to talk to someone.

Since Dan attended Calvary Temple, I decided to go back and continue facing the rejection that I had felt from the start. The first church activity I showed my face at was the single's hayride that following Saturday. Because I knew Dan would be there, I thought at least I would have someone to talk to or hide behind. Again, no one made an effort to talk with either one of us. I guess Dan didn't look any better than I did. Here he was at a single's event, though still married with kids, and going on a hayride with a young woman who was pregnant and ten years younger! I bet the gossip was going to be juicy, but I tried not to think about it. At least I had a friend to talk to. I don't think I would have continued to go to that church, let alone gone on that hayride, if Dan hadn't been there. Someone is better than no one, I thought. I wanted someone to rescue me.

Still searching for that supportive family and wanting to find my way back to God, I decided to join the choir. It was a big mistake. The pastor's wife was the choir director. Though she obviously noticed I was there, she didn't acknowledge me or welcome me back. Others would join or rejoin the choir for the Christmas program, and she would welcome them back by introducing them to the choir and giving them the opportunity to say a few words. Not me; I was completely ignored. If it wasn't for Jan, Marshal and Dan being in the choir, I may not have stayed. Although feeling like a complete outcast, I continued in the choir. Every week I came back and not once did the pastor's wife breathe one word to me.

Several times I would try to get an opportunity to speak with the pastor to ask him for advice or help, and he would just keep walking while I trailed behind him like a lost puppy. Not once did he turn to look at me or help me with any kind of guidance. He never inquired about my spiritual, emotional or physical needs; nor did he seem to care if I had a place to live. I was someone he did not want to deal with; I think he hoped I would just go away.

During that two to three-month period, I began working at a daycare across the street from the church. From Ruby's house it took almost thirty minutes to get there. That thirty minutes was time enough for me to think about my life and to shed many tears. But I had the comfort of a secure place to live until the baby was born and a job so I could save up some money.

Then one day I came home from work and Ruby had news for me. Ruby said that one of her relatives had died and she would be gone for several weeks, maybe even a month or two. Because her home was so far out in the country and I was four months into my pregnancy, she didn't want to risk something happening to me. I would need to find a new place within a couple of days.

My mind could scarcely comprehend what she was saying. Did she say I would have to find a place in a couple of days? But I'm so happy here… how could this be? I tried begging and pleading with her. I assured her that I would be fine. "Ruby, I'll be all right. Please, I can't move again." But Ruby's mind was made up and there was no negotiating. She insisted that it would be better if I had someone with me in case an emergency arose. I was filled with fear, shock, and hurt as I wondered where I would go next.

The distress of having to move again was almost unbearable. My blood pressure had been rising and was up considerably at my next visit to the doctor. Dr. Otto tried to cheer me up by making light of the situation. He joked about my moving adventures while holding up my chart and pointing to all the old addresses crossed off and the new ones scribbled in wherever they could fit. He would manage to put a smile on my face for a few minutes, but reality would set back in the minute I walked out the door.

Somehow…I don't remember how…I managed in those next two days to find a family who attended the same church that I did and who happened to live in one of the homes directly behind the church. They had one teenager living at home and another one who had already moved out. I was given the older one's vacant bedroom that included my own phone. The room was very small with barely enough room to walk around the bed. It was a far cry from what I had come from, but the family seemed very nice and the location couldn't have been better. I was able to walk to work and church within minutes. I was relieved and thankful to have a place to lay my head.

Within a couple of weeks of getting settled in my new home during the month of November, I had my first ultrasound. I had dreamed that I was walking hand in hand with a little dark-headed girl. I was hoping for a girl, because I was concerned that having a boy would only bring about more trouble from the father and remind me more of Nick than I wanted to remember. Nick had still been completely unsupportive up to that time, so I saw no reason why he should be part of our lives. He never helped financially or came to see me at any time during my pregnancy.

As I walked into the clinic, I breathed a prayer, "Please God, let it be a girl." I wanted someone to be there with me but here I was alone again. While I was sitting in the waiting room an uneasy feeling of self-consciousness came over me. I sat there fidgeting and wondering what people might be thinking about me. They probably didn't really notice or care, but I cared. With no ring on my finger signaling I was married and my pregnancy beginning to show, I was now another obvious statistic. Then my name was called: "Angela Stout." I moved quickly towards the nurse. "You're having an ultrasound today aren't you? Do you have anyone with you or is someone coming?" she asked. With my eyes down, I replied that no one was coming. I wanted to hide. Such an important event, having your first ultrasound, and normally an exciting time to share with someone, but I didn't have that privilege. The thrill of seeing the baby for the first time in the womb would have to be shared with the ultrasound technician.

After speaking briefly with the technician and answering a few questions, the ultrasound began. I lay there silently in the darkened room with my eyes fixed on the monitor. As the images came across the screen, the reality that there was a living human being in me began to sink in. In awe, I saw the tiny hands and feet and the baby's head — the baby was sucking his thumb. A tear trickled down my face as I thought, "Thank God I didn't get an abortion." I asked the technician if he knew if it was a boy or a girl, but he could not say because the doctor was the only one allowed to disclose that information. He did assure me that he was pretty sure of the baby's sex and that I could count on what the doctor would tell me. I left the room with ultrasound pictures in one hand while using the other hand to wipe away my tears.

While taking the elevator to the doctor's office on the second floor, my eyes were fixed on the photos of my unborn child. I could hardly wait to see Dr. Otto. When the doctor walked in the room, he had good news. "The baby looks healthy and has a strong heartbeat. Everything looks great." But he also said that it was important to keep my blood pressure down. I hadn't realized that the stress of everything I had been going through was affecting me so much. I thought I was handling it. I would always walk into Dr. Otto's office with a smile or a laugh. He enjoyed having me as a patient because of my happy countenance. However, it appeared that I was internalizing the turmoil that I had been facing on a daily basis. The doctor joked that my high blood pressure was due to having to come see him every month.

But now I wanted to know if the baby was a boy or a girl? Dr. Otto knew what I wanted. He looked over the report with a silly grin on his face that I could almost read. "It's a girl, isn't it!" I exclaimed. He turned with a smile and a sparkle in his eye, "Looks like you've got yourself a girl." "Yes! Thank you, Jesus!" I exclaimed. He tapped me assuredly with his folder and told me he'd see me again next month and not to get too stressed out.

When I got back to the house, I began showing the ultrasound picture to the family I was staying with and sharing my excitement over the baby being a girl. They said they were happy that I got my wish—they knew I had been hoping for a girl—but they didn't seem to share my enthusiasm. At that moment, I realized that I was quite possibly there for the purpose of teaching their teenage daughters that I was an example of what they didn't want them to do or be. Hence their lack of excitement.

I wanted someone to share this meaningful event with, someone that would be as excited as

I was. The loneliness I felt became a constant companion and any attention that I got I would completely soak up. The only person who seemed to care about what happened in my life was Dan. Dan and I had become good friends, mainly because he was there for me and he was concerned about my welfare. I had no one else to talk to, but I could always call him and he would be there for me. I could tell him anything. I don't know that I was much help to him in his situation, especially since I had never been married before and had never had children. But I was thankful that *someone* was there for me.

When I told him over the phone that the baby was a girl, he seemed genuinely happy for me. "That's great, I knew it would be a girl," he said. I told him that I would show him the ultrasound pictures later.

During this time, I turned to Dan more and more. I began mistaking my need for acceptance with a hope that somehow he was going to rescue me or help me find a way out of my embarrassment. We began to spend more time together, going to the park, grabbing a bite to eat, or watching TV at his place. Occasionally, I would have anxiety attacks, and he would stroke my temples as I closed my eyes to calm down. Since I didn't have support from anyone else,

I turned to Dan to share every bit of grief, loneliness, sadness, or hurt and any gleam of happiness that came my way. He would listen as I shared how I could not sleep at night because my nerves felt like they were jumping and crawling inside of me and I would get up out of my bed in the middle of the night to literally shake out the nerves. He knew of my struggles regarding whether I should go up to Kansas City and give the baby up for adoption because I felt so incapable of raising a child at this time in my life. I needed a good friend to confide in and that's what I got. At times, we would talk for hours, or I'd fall asleep, so that sometimes I went home late. In any case, I didn't look forward to going back to a place where I didn't feel completely wanted.

One of those nights, I came back to the house particularly late. Both Dan and I had dozed off to sleep in the living room and didn't realize that it was almost one o'clock in the morning. Dan rushed me back to the house. The house was dark, so I was startled when Donna's voice called to me from the couch to come and sit down so she could talk to me. "What time is it?" she asked sleepily. When I told her, she wanted to know what Dan and I could possibly be doing out so late. I was hurt by what she was implying, but I understood why she had to ask. I told her how Dan was the only friend I could talk to and that we just fell asleep in his living room watching TV and didn't realize the time. She said that she understood that he was a good friend, but her blood pressure was going up. "Why? Because of me staying out late?" I asked with great concern. "No," she responded. "It's the church."

"What do you mean?"

"Well, the church owns the house and they want you to get out," she replied.

A rush of horror came over me and my heart pounded harder. "Why? What have I done now? I've asked for forgiveness. I'm doing the best I can! What more do they want from me?"

"I don't know." Her voice softened. "They just want you out. Angela, they have been saying terrible things about you behind your back. Just be careful who you talk to."

I was absolutely shocked. Numbness set in. "So when do I need to be out by?" I was afraid to ask.

"Tomorrow," she said without emotion.

"Tomorrow?!! Where am I going to go? I exhausted every possible resource before. How could I possibly find a place by tomorrow? Where could I go so quickly?" My desperation at that moment was profound.

"I don't know," she replied apologetically.

"Can't you give me until the weekend? That will give me some time to look for someone to stay with." I begged.

"I can't. You don't know the pressure I'm under from the church. It has to be tomorrow. Angela, there's nothing else I can do. We don't own this house, the church does. We have no choice."

There was nothing else to say. I walked back to my temporary room, feeling completely hopeless once again. I didn't know where I would be twenty-four hours from that moment. I felt destroyed inside. How could I go back to the church and face everyone? Who could I trust? Who was acting friendly to my face but whispering behind my back? I felt even more alone than ever.

Daylight came too soon after a sleepless night. The only person that I knew to call was Dan. When I notified him of my situation, he offered to help me move my belongings out of the house and he said I could stay in a spare bedroom until I found another place. With tears in my eyes, I began packing. I could hardly face the family. I didn't even want to look at them. I was overwhelmed and consumed by hurt. I could hardly talk as the hours slowly ticked by while I waited for Dan to get off work. The only thing I knew was that at least I would have a place to lay my head that night. After that, I did not know what might befall me. Where would I be for the next few months? When Dan arrived and started loading up my belongings, Donna had the nerve to ask me where I would be going. I'm sure she had her ideas and if I mentioned I was staying at Dan's that night, gossip would run rampant. Who knows…maybe I couldn't trust them either! Besides, this was going to be a temporary stay and I still had no idea where I would end up. I thought to myself, 'How dare they ask me that when I only had a few hours to even get out of their home!" But my rapid fire emotions always circled back to the painful loneliness.

Numbly I said, "I don't know. I have no idea."

Dan finished packing and once again I was out the door with a few half-hearted hugs and goodbyes. I didn't know what was going on behind the scenes with the church, but I was sure there was something more wrong than she had told me.

When we arrived at Dan's house, we discreetly brought in a few of my belongings. We knew this did not look good and I really wanted to do the right thing. He still was not divorced and here I was, a young pregnant woman moving my belongings into his house. But I had no other choice with such short notice. Despite having a roof over my head and a friend who was supportive, this was about the lowest time I had in all those difficult months: the *feeling* of being rejected by the church was replaced by *knowing* I was rejected by the church.

Knowing I needed to quickly find another place to stay, the next morning I began my search by making calls to the Crisis Pregnancy Center and Cornerstone Church as they had been instrumental in helping me find Ruby, whom I had stayed with previously. They asked me if I had checked with my own church for help, and it made me feel terrible that I had to go outside of my own church for support. Fortunately, Cornerstone's church secretary, Myra, knew of a single mother I might be able to stay with if I would be willing to help look after her two-year-old daughter. Myra said she would check into it and get back to me.

Several days went by and I still had not heard from Myra. I hated the fact that if anyone found out I was staying with Dan, there was no doubt what they would think. I knew we weren't doing anything wrong and we both had our own rooms. I was doing the best I could under the circumstances, and I was trying hard to find another place.

In the meantime, the Christmas program at the church was that following weekend. I decided, as did Dan, to tough it out and stay with the choir until the program was over. Both of us had gone faithfully to all the practices and, as for me, there was no way I was going to not show up because of what others thought. I was looking forward to the weekend being over with though, because I was planning to leave the church and never return once the last song was sung. There was no doubt that the choir director and the choir members were astonished when they saw that I was not quitting. Because of what Donna had said, I was careful who I spoke with, and even when I did speak I chose my words carefully.

When the night of the program arrived, I began to feel a sense of relief, knowing that my time there was just about over. I couldn't wait to get out of the church. And Dan, disappointed at how I had been treated, decided he would not go back either. When the last note was sung and the applause ended, and the pastor finished the final prayer, I walked out of the church and never looked back.

A few days later, I got a call from Sheri, the single mother who Myra had referred me to for a place to stay. We agreed that I would stay with her free in exchange for some baby-sitting on the side. The only problem was that I couldn't move in for two weeks until her roommate moved out. I asked her to please let me know if something happened and I could move in sooner. In the meantime, I continued to check around for any other possibilities since I did not want to burden Dan any longer.

The next few Sundays, we visited several churches together. I made an appointment with one of the pastors for some counseling, which I so needed. I remember his harsh tone and how belittled I felt. When I told him about Dan, his reply was, "why don't you marry him then, if he cares about you?" The advice was not for my benefit but more for the sake of appearance. I wasn't seeking marriage. I was seeking wisdom and insight to help guide me regarding what I should do next. I left feeling bad about myself; clearly this place would not be my church home either.

In the midst of searching for a church, I moved in with Sheri and her daughter and began receiving government aid. So at least I had food and shelter; what I now needed was to find a loving and caring church where I could find some healing and peace.

One Wednesday night in February, I visited a church called Rolling Hills. I had heard about it before and I had even talked briefly with their church counselor, Kevin, on the phone. Kevin said that the church might be able to help me pay my first month's rent for an apartment if I promised to pay them back when I was able. Kevin encouraged me to come and visit the church. I had hesitated about going there because of my past experiences, but I was at the end of the rope.

So here I was, seven months pregnant, walking into the church. The service had exuberant worship and the people there seemed to genuinely enjoy praising God, dancing with hands uplifted. The pastor preached a biblically sound and wonderful message. I was thoroughly touched by the warmth and friendliness there. After the service, I stood anxiously toward the front of the church where Kevin was so I could let him know that I had come there. Not knowing what he looked like, I walked up to Pastor Mike to ask where I could find Kevin. As I approached, the pastor bent down from the platform and reached out to shake my hand. I told him that I was here to see Kevin and I began to explain my situation. Tears began to well up in my eyes, perhaps out of fear of being rejected again.

Then, unlike what I had experienced from other pastors, he spoke softly and with compassion as he looked right at me and said, "Let me pray for you,

Angela." I nodded and he placed his hand on my arm and began praying. I don't remember anything else in his prayer except the words, "I bind all condemnation in the name of Jesus."

They were words I had been longing to hear. For the first time since becoming pregnant, I felt a sense of relief, peace and freedom. I realized that what had been happening to me was condemnation—by pastors, church people, and uncaring and unforgiving individuals, including myself. I had asked for God's forgiveness, but His forgiveness was not made real in my life until that moment. The song, "There is therefore now no condemnation to those who are in Christ Jesus," based on Romans 8:1, became my theme song. A great burden had been lifted and I could now concentrate on the last two months of my pregnancy.

Soon after the pastor's prayer, we were able to locate Kevin. Kevin and I talked briefly and he assured me that they'd be more than willing to help. We set up an appointment and I went to his office to talk with him the next day. Stepping into the office that day had a different feel than anything that had gone before. Everyone was pleasant and genuinely helpful. Not one negative thought came to me as I spoke with Kevin that day. We discussed what I had been going through and my plans for an apartment and expenses. Before I left, we agreed that when I had made a final decision on the apartment I would let him know so they could help me.

Back at Sheri's duplex, I was being treated unfairly. Somehow, Sheri felt that her status of being a model and making money allowed her to treat me as a lesser being. I was a homeless girl on food stamps and Medicaid. I took care of myself, though, bought my own food, helped with utilities, kept the place clean, and babysat her daughter all day while she was at work. But soon she began leaving her daughter with me more often and expecting more from me in other ways. It wasn't just during the day she wanted me to watch her toddler, but now she was asking for nights and weekends while she went out on dates and out on the town with friends.

What topped it all off was when I'd come home minutes before she did one Sunday after church and found dog excrement all over the floor. She had "forgotten" to put her huge Golden Retriever away and he had a major accident. When she came in and saw the "dog doo" on the floor she immediately went into a rage asking me why I hadn't cleaned it up. At seven months into my pregnancy, I was barely able to get close enough to stand the smell without wanting to vomit, let alone having to pick it up in my state. I knew at that point things were only bound to get worse and I knew I had to find a way to get out of there soon.

I quickly enlisted Dan's help and we planned that the next Sunday after church I would leave Sheri's house and stay with Dan until I got my apartment. And that's what we did. I gave her no warning and no notice so I wouldn't have any problems with her. I knew it wasn't a good choice to be at Dan's again, but again I was backed up against the wall with no place to go. Plus I knew that it would only be a couple of weeks before I found the apartment I wanted.

In my search for an apartment, I was drawn back to the same apartment complex that I had lived in before and that I was most familiar with. The apartments were well-kept with a swimming pool and good management. Joy, the manager, told me that children normally weren't allowed, but she would let me come on board for a year. After a year, I would have to look for another place. I was not concerned with that stipulation because I was so happy to have a place of my own where I could settle down securely before the baby arrived. My dad helped me with the deposit and Rolling Hills helped me with the first month's rent.

In March, one month before I was to have the baby, I moved into the one-bedroom apartment. My apartment was empty for only a short time before I received gifts of furniture. One of Dan's co-workers gave to me a wood framed couch and matching chair that were in excellent condition. She also found tucked away in her attic a large metal dining table. Little by little, my empty shell of an apartment turned into a home. Dan had a baby bed in his shed that his children had used. We fixed it up, painted it, and set it up in the bedroom. With the baby bed in place, and my new furniture and other basic necessities, I felt that at last I was "nesting."

I was now able to completely focus on getting prepared for the baby. Food and healthcare were no longer an issue either since I was receiving welfare checks, food stamps, and Medicaid. To make up for an occasional shortage of cash, my dad would send some money to help out. Because I didn't have much to give back but I did have plenty of food, I often invited those who helped me over for dinner as a way of saying "thank you."

I no longer had to wonder where I was going to live the next day, no imposing upon other people's homes, and no more searching for a loving and caring church.

I had found a home in every aspect of life: a good doctor, a loving friend, my own apartment, and my spiritual family—the church. I also began to have some peace within my own heart. Without the help of those around me, though, I would never have experienced this. And to all those who cared enough, I owe the deepest gratitude.

CHAPTER THREE
Having Baby

With only a few weeks left before the birth, my parents came down—a 10-hour trip for them by car—with the rest of my belongings. They hoped the baby would arrive while they were there, but the days came and went with no sign of imminent delivery.

At some point, my parents felt that they needed to go back home. I knew it was futile to beg them to stay longer; they were ready to go back. I somehow felt it was my fault that I didn't have the baby while they were there. When they left, I experienced that familiar empty, lonely feeling that had been with me throughout my pregnancy.

During this time, Nick got in contact with me to ask if he could come when the baby was born. The nerve of this guy to leave me alone for nine months and then suddenly decide it's time to appear and see the baby! My doctor could not believe Nick's proposition either, and was glad when I refused to let Nick have any part of the delivery process. The thought of Nick having free reign to do as he pleased for the past nine months and offering no support to me while I struggled tremendously — and then to show up and play the "I'm the daddy" role — made me furious. The only positive outcome I could foresee if I did allow him to come to the hospital is that I would be assured of not being alone.

In the meantime, Dan was finalizing his own divorce proceedings and found joy in helping me through this rough time in my life. When Dan's home sold and he had to get an apartment, he rented a town home opposite to mine. Soon after he moved in, we found out that the upstairs hallway of his apartment was the back wall of my kitchen. We developed a system of knocks when we needed something or to signal that the other was ready to leave. He became the friend I could lean on. I do not recollect any other friends following up with me on a regular basis or even on a sporadic basis. But Dan was there and I began to get very dependent upon him.

The days came and went right on past my due date. Dr. Otto planned to induce labor on April 3.

The timing must have been part of God's divine plan, because I went into labor on my own early that morning. Fortunately, Dan was able to take the day off work and get me to the hospital. I was relieved during my labor to know that I would not be alone all day and that Dan would stay through the delivery. Sadly, though, no one else came to visit during the long labor hours. I knew that if Dan hadn't been there, no one would have been there. I couldn't think of anything worse than being alone while having my baby.

The hours came and went. Labor was long and hard. None of the medications worked for me, including the epidural. After twenty-two hours of labor, the baby was stressed and I was in pain and exhausted. When I asked the nurse how much longer it might be, she didn't have a clear answer. She commented on how long it had taken me to dilate this far and that it would be hard to estimate how much longer it might be before I would be ready to deliver. A short time later, they decided to do an emergency C-section. I was afraid, especially because my doctor was not on call that night. My next immediate concern was whether Dan would be able to go into the operating room since we were not related. Maybe they felt sorry for me because there was no one else there, so they let him come in with me.

They wheeled my bed in the delivery room and the doctor that had come in to deliver my baby was not very pleasant with me. I got the impression that he was unhappy because it was 2 am, I was not his patient, I was a Medicaid patient, and I was a single soon-to-be mom. I knew there were a couple of different types of C-section cuts, so I blurted out that I wanted a bikini cut. He quickly snapped, "Why? You won't be able to wear a bikini anyway with the stretchmarks you've got." Silence fell on the room amongst the nurses and those assisting with the delivery. I was stunned too. There I was laid out on the cold metal table being prepped for a cesarean, to be cut open by a doctor who was not showing the best of manners and patient care. I laid there silent and frightened as a tear rolled down the side of my face.

When the doctor opened me up and saw the baby he commented that the baby had lots of hair and tried to lighten things up by joking that the hair was the cause of the baby not being able to come out because the hair was tangled up around my pelvis. Then a few minutes later, I heard the sound…the cry of my baby and someone announcing, "It's a girl!"

They bathed her, wrapped her up in a blanket,

and handed her to Dan so I could look at her. I was elated at how beautiful she was. Her dark, almost black hair stood thick and long, so much so that the nurses were able to swirl a huge curl on top of her head. She had gorgeous olive skin and cocoa-colored, almond-shaped eyes. I was awed by her perfection. Dan said, "Isn't she beautiful?" I nodded while gazing at the tiny human being that was part of me.

As they finished the surgery, the nurses began their routine check-up of Kayla. They found her healthy and strong and brought her to me in the recovery room. Those first few moments of nursing her were precious moments and I soaked in the joy of it all.

Soon the nurses came to take her to the nursery and I was moved to the room where I would be for the remainder of my stay. Dan came with me and I asked him if he would stay until he had to leave for work in a few hours. He checked with the hospital staff and they allowed him to stay in the chair. I was exhausted and at the same time still afraid to be alone. As I fell asleep, I wondered how I was going to handle this new thing of being a mom. The sleep was restless and short lived; it was time for Dan to leave for work. He contacted the church to let the pastors know the good news and I made a few calls home. My family couldn't wait to see the first photos.

I was looking forward to being with my little baby girl. When the nurses brought her to me, I felt very awkward handling her at first. But soon holding Kayla became second nature. I was awed by her beauty and even more so by her vulnerability. I was suddenly struck by the vast sense of responsibility I had for caring for her and raising her. I knew that by myself I could not do it. God would have to be my constant source of strength and help for whatever lay ahead.

Later that day, Linda, the pastor's wife, came to see me. I was surprised when she walked through the door with beautiful roses for me. I had low expectations when it came to receiving visits from the church since I was just a new attendee. Joy welled up in my heart as she told me how beautiful Kayla was. Linda, with such grace, spoke lovingly and gently to me. I was touched that she took the time to talk with me and pray over me and my baby. When she left, I felt a sense of peace knowing that I had found a church family that truly cared about me.

Outside of Dan and Linda, there were only a few visitors. Every now and then I would feel the sting of not having a family member around for support. I kept on doing what I had to do and Dan was the one who was available more than anyone else in my life.

The day came when I had to give the information for Kayla's birth certificate. I had questioned over and over in my mind as to whether I should have Nick's name put on the birth certificate for the father or not. When the nurse routinely asked for the father's name, I was silent. Then I told her to put nothing. "Just leave it blank. Can you leave it blank?" I asked. She looked up at me quizzically. "You don't know who the father is?" "Yes I do know who the father is. I just don't want any problems from him." She tried to persuade me to name him, stating that it would be helpful because he could be forced to pay child support. I still refused to give her the name. Afterward, I wondered if I had done the right thing, but I didn't want to give him credit by naming him as the father when he hadn't acted and prepared like a father should. Yes, he should have to pay support, but at the same time I didn't want trouble with visits from him for all of Kayla's childhood.

After three days in the hospital, it was time for

Kayla and me to go home. I didn't know whether to look forward to it or dread it. Certainly I was excited about getting back to my own home, but I knew that going home meant that I would be alone and without much help with my newborn. I hadn't had much experience with newborns—only preschoolers when I helped out in daycares. How could I be a good mother? What would happen next in our lives? How would I be able to support the both of us long-term? I felt insecure and knew I would have little help.

Dan, as usual, was there to pick up Kayla and me at the hospital. I dressed Kayla in a pretty pink dress, pink booties, and a matching headband—a gorgeous way to be introduced to the world. A nurse commented that she looked like a little Indian. They didn't know that her biological grandmother was of Spanish decent. Kayla's complexion was a result of that heritage.

As the nurse wheeled me out in the wheelchair with me holding Kayla, the compliments continued to pour in regarding her beauty and "all that hair." When we reached the car, the nurse showed me how to properly place Kayla in the car seat and assisted me to sit next to her. I waved goodbye to the hospital staff, at the same time longing for them to come home with me to help me adjust to my new life.

Driving home, Dan and I talked about the events of the past few days. As we arrived at the apartment, excitement swelled in me at the thought of bringing my daughter home to the place I had prepared for her. I thought, "That must be how the heavenly Father feels about bringing us to the heavenly home He has prepared for us." Ready for Kayla's arrival was the baby bed decorated with little lamb sheets and a comforter, a crate filled with baby toys, and various gifts including diapers and clothing from a baby shower given to me by Jan. Kayla was peacefully sleeping as I placed her in the bed for the first time. As I was still sore from the C-section, Dan helped me lower her into the crib. Then we quietly walked out of the room and worked on settling me in, so I could get around on my own without much help. We moved the glasses, plates and bowls lower in the cupboard so I wouldn't have to reach while I was still recovering. I appreciated Dan's help and dreaded when he left. It's not easy for any new mom, let alone one that has to do it all by herself, but somehow I would have to be strong. That afternoon, while I was rocking Kayla, my dad called. He was checking on me to see how we were doing. Everything was fine, but tears began to stream down my face when I shared, from my deep well of thoughts, how glad I was that I hadn't aborted her or given her away. I would have never known or held this precious soul or seen the beauty God could create from my sin. God does forgive. God does give grace to those He has humbled (Proverbs 3:34, James 4:6). At that moment, I felt an overwhelming sense of peace and gratitude for my decision to not do the unthinkable (have an abortion) and I trusted in the Divine to help me raise my little daughter.

Within a couple of weeks, a group from church gave me a small baby shower. They had a beautiful cake, mints, and punch set up on a decorated table for me. I brought Kayla in and they lovingly held her, listened to my story, and prayed for us. The group pulled together funds and bought a baby swing that I had been wanting. As Kayla got a little bigger, it allowed her to enjoy the rocking motion while watching me cook a meal or do household chores. I also found as the weeks went by that she was a colicky baby. And while the swing helped a little, I was increasingly having a hard time finding ways to soothe her.

Kayla's colic became worse as the days turned into weeks and weeks turned into months. She would cry most of the night. I knew nothing about colicky babies but I was learning fast that there wasn't much I could do. I would rock her for a long time but nothing would console her. I was exhausted from the nightly constant crying, but I wasn't the only one not sleeping; the noise was also disturbing the neighbors. One night, the man came over in the middle of the night when Kayla was crying and asked me if I could move my baby into another room of the apartment because he and his wife couldn't sleep. I was not only surprised at his suggestion, since I thought he might be offering help, but I was offended. I didn't have any other rooms. I had taken her away from the bedroom that was up against their wall and had been bringing her into the living room. There were no neighbors on that side, but they could still hear her. Upset and with the baby crying, I called Dan and he came over to walk her in the stroller. After a while, he returned with Kayla sound asleep. He said he had ended up taking her for a drive in the car because the stroller didn't calm her down at all.

Now that the neighbors were complaining, I was now more on edge about her crying. I was afraid they would say something to the manager and I would be asked to leave. Thankfully, time passed and so did the colic.

The first step I was looking forward to making was having my daughter dedicated to the Lord. One Sunday morning, the church was having a baby dedication. I was the only single mother amongst the couples that stood before the church that day, but I stood there proudly with my beautiful daughter. Once again, it was an awkward moment for me but I was determined to do what I felt was right. The pastor announced the parents and their babies' names. Several elders in the church were called upfront to anoint and pray for the babies while the pastor led the congregation in prayer. Kayla was especially blessed when one of the deacons who did not know that she had already been anointed with the oil, came over and anointed her a second time on her tiny forehead. I had to smile to think that she was given a double anointing!

I also began singing again. Eddie and Charlene, a couple I knew from college, asked me to come and sing a few songs at a nursing home they were ministering in. Kayla was about two months old and they encouraged me to bring her with me. When I sang for the elderly that day, I sang with more gratitude and praise than ever before, and with a deeper appreciation for the grace of God. Afterwards, several senior citizens gathered around to see the precious little baby I had brought with me. Most of them hadn't seen a baby in years. One feeble woman began to shed tears as she held Kayla. Charlene looked at me and said, "See Angela, she's going to be a blessing."

CHAPTER FOUR
Moving On

Every moment and event became special as I watched Kayla grow. I remember my first Mother's Day. I dressed Kayla up in a beautiful ruffled yellow dress with a matching bow. The color made her dark hair and olive skin stand out. Kayla was my Mother's Day gift and I couldn't wait to proudly take her to church that morning. I didn't have to hang my head in shame because I was a single mom. At Rolling Hills, there was an understanding that all children are a blessing and God is the giver of life. Bursting with joy over my little one, I stood up with all the other mothers that were acknowledged that day. I even received my first Mother's Day flowers, bought by Dan and signed, "Love, Kayla."

As for singing and ministry—well, I thought that aspect of my life would be null and void. Then the music director gave me the opportunity to sing a solo. I realized that God was being extremely merciful to me for I truly did not deserve anything, or so I felt. Shortly after singing the solo, I was asked to be a part of the Praise Team. The Praise Team was a group of about five singers that assisted the worship leader in praise and worship. My heart was exhilarated at the opportunity, and God continued to confirm to me time and time again that He wasn't through with me yet as I continued to minister in song and with the team over the next few years. God blessed me as I walked in the path. He opened new doors for me to use the talents He had given.

As the summer months progressed, Dan's divorce proceedings heated and became unbearable for him. At one point, in exasperation, Dan said he didn't care if everything he owned was taken from him. In July, the divorce became final and he was not left with much. Dan, relieved of the pressures he had been dealing with for over four years, was able to get more involved in the church. I was happy for him that he was growing as a person. My feelings for him were only those of friendship, yet I depended on him so heavily — too heavily.

In August, I began working for a local company in shipping and had a sense of accomplishment in that I was able to provide a little for Kayla and me. Dan worked a different shift than I did, and because I was unable to afford childcare, Dan looked after Kayla while I was at work. He treated her as well as any father could and would often bring her to visit me on my breaks at work so I could spend time with her. I don't know how I would have managed without his help and friendship. Because of his bonding with Kayla, I began to wonder how I could move on from the relationship. I felt I had a sense of obligation to him for all that he had done for me, and I loved him as a friend, but I did not see myself marrying him. Yet I wrestled with the thought of how a Bible College graduate could afford to raise a child by herself without much or any support. There were no simple answers. Here was someone who genuinely cared for my daughter and me, and though I appreciated him so much, I didn't think of him as a lifelong partner.

At this point, Dan was hired by another manufacturing company with more pay and better benefits. One of the benefits was adoption coverage. He brought up the possibility of adopting Kayla. Of course, he would be a wonderful father. He already *was* a wonderful father. But was he *the one* for me? Questions swirled in my mind and I was completely confused. As a single mom, I felt trapped by my own circumstances and I needed support. While something inside of me was saying, "No, don't do it," circumstances were saying, "What choice do you have? How can you make it on your own? This way, you'll be able to spend more time with Kayla." In my quandary, I asked my brother and sister-in-law about the situation. I explained that he was "just" a friend. Looking back, that alone should have been a big red flag for me. But the response from them was, "What better thing could you do than marry your best friend." "I guess," I responded uncertainly.

In December, we came to the conclusion that we should get married—a logical decision for me. There was virtually no intimacy before the wedding—not even kissing, because I couldn't give that to him. He didn't think anything of it, since my excuse was that I was waiting until we were married. But the truth was…I couldn't see myself with him like that. I was given a bridal shower and when I was asked if I would like "something special… you know…to wear for the honeymoon," my mind wasn't there at all. I could tell my response was not what was expected for someone who should be in love and looking forward to spending time alone with her loved one.

Some friends are meant to stay as friends. Not

every open door is meant to be walked through and when you have as many internal warning signals as I did, those signals should be heeded.

After an uneventful expected proposal, the disappointment in my heart set in. This is not how I wanted my life to be...not the proposal, not the wedding, not any of this. The crash course I was taking to the altar had begun and, for me, I didn't know how I could turn back. Even Dan's parents were skeptical of us as much as I was of them. His mom noted something that she could have only read in my personal journal while I was away from home and they were visiting—another sign that I was heading in the wrong direction.

Every notion I had ever had of having a summer wedding quickly vanished as we announced a cold January wedding date. Preparations were started immediately for the fittings, cake, church reservations, and wedding ceremony, along with the pastor to perform it. There wasn't much time to prepare because it was December and Christmas was coming, and the wedding right after that. We managed to enjoy Christmas—I got my first live tree, seven feet high and almost hitting the ceiling in my small apartment. Strung with white lights, homemade popcorn garlands, and a few ornaments, including Kayla's first Christmas ornament, the beauty and fragrance of the tree brought an added joy to the season, while at the same time busying my mind so I didn't have to think about the upcoming wedding. The only bump in the road was when another church member came to me and told me, "Angela you know you are not doing the right thing by marrying him." I thought, "What does she know? She doesn't know me!" Yet in my heart I knew she was right. At the same time, everything was falling into place. How could I stop it now? I didn't have the courage.

The Christmas season was barely over when the wedding date arrived. The night before the wedding, I was extremely restless. When I did sleep, I had a nightmare. I dreamed that I was walking down the aisle knowing I was marrying the wrong person. As I neared the altar, I woke up, startled, and sat straight up in my bed. I exclaimed, "Oh, my God, I am making the biggest mistake of my life!"

I worked at reasoning with myself. "That was only a dream. Pastor Mike is marrying us and I know that everything is all right and it will be okay." I sincerely believed that Pastor Mike was a man of God and I knew that his presence would be a confirmation or blessing of the marriage. Having had very little sleep, I got up and began the preparations for the day. As I was gathering items to go to my hair and makeup appointment, the phone rang. When I answered, I was surprised to hear the voice at the other end. It was Pastor Mike! In a raspy, voice, he said…"Angela, I am so sorry. I cannot perform your wedding today; I am sick." My head swirled. "You can't?" I didn't know what to say. He told me that Kevin would be officiating the wedding. Kevin was supposed to be one of the best men at the wedding. I don't understand why I didn't call the wedding off right at that moment. Maybe it was the embarrassment of having the church already set up and the expenses that came with it; or maybe it was the fear of not knowing how I'd make it alone. Again, I rationalized. I told myself that the substitution had already been made, that it was only a minor adjustment, and that everything would go on as planned.

I went to my friend's home and had my hair and makeup done by her husband who was a professional makeup artist. I focused on getting ready and didn't have much to say. After receiving a last minute blessing from my friends, I drove alone to the church. I began muttering to myself. "I know I may be making a big mistake, but at least my daughter will have a daddy. He will be a good father and our needs will be met." I didn't turn back.

My daughter was gorgeous, sitting up in her burgundy and white ruffled dress as she was being escorted down the aisle in front of me in a small red wagon. As the wedding march began, I wrapped my arm over my dad's arm and I knew as we walked down the aisle that I was making the biggest mistake of my life. The warning signs had been blaring at me, but I had chosen not to listen. There were tears that day from both sides, but my tears were tears of regret.

After the ceremony and the opening of the gifts from the small number of attendees, the guests lined up to cheer us on. And there we were alone together in the car on the way to our honeymoon. I found myself dreading what was to happen next. I tried to pretend that I was okay, but I was not. When we arrived at the hotel thirty minutes later, I was numb. We got everything settled in the hotel room and I dutifully began to prepare myself for what was about to happen. I grabbed my negligee and headed to the bathroom. I took my time putting it on. My mind was racing. How could I get out of this one? But there was no way. I kept shaking my head: "I can't do this. I can't do this." That night, as sad as it was, I could not wait until it was over. I wanted to run but there was nowhere to hide. I felt as if I was being raped, even though that is not what happened. Some friends were meant to be just friends.

We continued our journey. The first thing we sought to get done was for Dan to officially adopt Kayla. Although Nick was not on the birth certificate and had not supported me and Kayla in any way, the attorney wanted to cover all bases and make sure the adoption was clean. Nick had lived in Missouri for a short time after college and apparently had a new partner. When we finally caught up with Nick, our attorney pressed Nick to sign a consent form to release his parental rights. With his consent, we were allowed to fully proceed with Dan's adoption of Kayla. By the time the adoption process was finalized, Kayla was 1½ years old. With the adoption came the name change and now we felt more like an official family.

The first couple of years, I tried to overcome my lack of intimate feelings towards Dan. After all, he was a good man and father. Then, when Kayla was about 2½ years old, I became pregnant. I was so happy to have a sibling for her, and I was elated when I found out, via the ultrasound, that the baby was a boy. When Seth was born, he added a new element of joy to our lives.

I turned my focus on the children and the attention they needed. I enjoyed being a stay-at-home mom and baking goodies and playing games with them. My time with the children allowed me to forget about the loneliness I was feeling inside. We took normal family vacations and enjoyed cook-outs and bonfires with friends when we lived in the country. But Dan and I never interacted intimately, not even a kiss or a peck on the cheek in front of the children. I often wondered how this might affect them—not seeing their parents loving each other.

And when the children were in bed and the world seemed to stop, I was back alone with my thoughts, in my own bed, wondering if this was how my life would be.

CHAPTER FIVE

Depression

Where do I begin with a chapter titled "Depression?" I believe the downhill trend began when I said, "I do," but now I was in it and there seemed to be no escape. I involved myself in as many aspects of ministry as I could, and I did my best to have the appearance of the perfect family while all hell was breaking loose at home.

As I got to know Dan more, I found we were far from compatible in many areas—not only physically, but intellectually and spiritually. We were not sleeping in the same bed; we didn't have anything to talk about when we were alone; and we didn't seem to be connected spiritually outside of the fact that we were at the same church. I was also handling the finances as best as I could, because he was not good at managing them.

My mind was constantly tormented by thoughts

of "What if I hadn't...?" or "Oh, my life is wasted...." or "I'll never be happy because I'll never know what it is to really love someone...." or "what would the ministry have been like...?" I was constantly tripped up by "what could have been." I was wrought with such pain about the past that at times I thought my heart would literally break. In a journal entry dated December 10, 1994, I wrote:

> *"Here I am steeped in depression, tears well up in me and my heart hurts so bad. All I can say is that loneliness and hurt have always gripped my heart, but even so more today. If it weren't for my children, I don't think I'd be here today. And no one can ever help me. No one. What's the use — no one could understand the pain."*

Suicidal thoughts plagued me in my deepest moments of pain. I felt trapped in my useless life with nowhere to turn. I replayed every painful event from my childhood that I could remember. From not feeling good enough to be successful...to hurts inflicted on me by others...to my own failures that brought me to that point in my life. The warning from the church member, the dream the night before the wedding day, and the pastor not being able to perform the wedding for us ran through my mind, solidifying my stupid mistakes. I hadn't listened. I hadn't listened to the Voice. I knew that Voice and I ignored it. Though the pain was unbearable, I could not take my life. That was not my choice to make because I had children that needed me. I believed that I would live out a life that would be miserable until the end.

Depression also played a part in my anger. I was angry because I had no way out. I was angry at what others did to me. I was angry at Nick for getting to go on with his life and doing whatever he wanted while I lived through this hell. I was angry at myself for the bad choices that I had made. I was angry that whatever God had wanted me to do was most likely gone forever. I was angry that I would never be a full-time minister. I was angry that my future lacked any hope.

Now, as I think over some of the episodes of my angry outbursts, I am ashamed. At times, I was so miserable inside that I vented my ugliness in front of my family. I remember an outrageous moment when I simply "lost it," grabbing a large, full six-foot bookcase and pulling it to the ground, scattering books everywhere and knocking down anything else in my path. As if that wasn't bad enough, my children were now standing at the door and Seth asked what was wrong with me. My outrage came to a quick halt and I walked away.

While all this was going on, I was still going to church and I still had no one in my life to help me with the pain. I'm not sure if I would have been able to tell anyone what was going on, since I didn't want to be rejected again. All the crying at night, the tears that soaked the pillow beneath my head and the loneliness…no one knew except God. My spirit would tell me that God saw my tears—every one. But then I would ask, "How long, Lord?" "How long do I have to suffer for my sin?" "How long do I have to pay for my mistakes?" "Is this how I am to live the rest of my life?" "Is this all there is?" And when I questioned, there was only silence…no answers.

One day I confided to a woman at church. She lifted my spirits by offering me a simple parable: "Angela, if one of your children broke a vase and asked you for forgiveness, you'd say, 'Yes, I forgive you—be more careful next time.' But what if that child, two weeks later, came back crying and said, 'Mommy, I'm sorry for breaking that vase two weeks ago. Please forgive me.' You'd say, 'Honey, I've already forgiven you. It's okay. It's over with.' But then the child comes back a month later, five months later and one year later, asking forgiveness over that same vase that he broke a long time ago. Then you'd probably be exasperated and say, "Look, honey, I have forgiven you a long time ago. I have forgotten about it. Now will you get on with your life and forget about the vase?'"

It was so simple and so true! God must be tired of my constant moaning over past sins! She told me that God would work with me according to where I was at this time, and that God was not surprised by the decisions I had made. She said, "God knew what was going to happen in your life. He doesn't have plan A, B, and C, and then if A doesn't work out, well, oops, we'll move on to plan B and so on. No! God does not work like that."

I felt relieved and uplifted.

Dan and I had also begun attending a new church after our pastor had left. I approached the new pastor regarding our marriage. He told me to stay in the marriage and God would give me the love for my husband. And he told me that he didn't believe that it was over for me as far as being in ministry. He encouraged me and I thought I would at least try.

Though nothing really changed at home, I began to be more heavily involved at church. I participated in lead roles in church musicals, became a Praise

Team ensemble member, and sang anointed solos. I had given encouraging words to the entire church body. I had been the church receptionist and was later promoted to be one of the pastor's secretaries. But outside of the church, my family life was increasingly miserable.

Not only was the marriage not there, but we were having problems with our rebellious teenage daughter. There were many things going on that neither I nor Dan knew how to handle.

Dan's way of dealing with her behavior was to try to bring some kind of peace to the situation, whereas I would try to discipline her. Neither approach seemed to work, and we were particularly at a loss when her angry behavior escalated to violence.

As a young teenager, Kayla was beautiful, athletic, wonderful with children (as demonstrated by her love of teaching gymnastics), and an inspired pianist. She was amazingly creative when it came to fashion and drawing clothing designs.

But as she got older, she became rebellious and angry and violent. I looked back and wondered what had happened to that adorable girl who loved to draw pictures and play with her brother. Did we somehow fail as parents to nurture her wonderful strengths? Was it something to do with our uncon-

ventional marriage? Or was it more the rebellious-
ness of a teenager with a strong and determined
personality?

 Whatever it was, I was shocked by her rage and
I had no idea what to do. Certainly I didn't handle
myself well. I said horrible things to her that I have
asked forgiveness for over and over again.

Besides that, Kayla always felt that Seth was fa-
vored, particularly since she wasn't Dan's biological child and Seth was. Yet I absolutely loved them
equally and I know that Dan did also — he had been
Kayla's father since the moment she was born. We
gave Kayla so many opportunities to succeed at
anything she wanted to try — piano, gymnastics, ice
skating, and dancing, but she was still jealous.

We tried family counseling with three different
Christian counselors, but it didn't help the situation.
One counselor commented that Kayla was a pow-
erhouse and that maybe one day she'd be a power-
house for God.

I was also experiencing difficulties with
Dan's mother. When Kayla was a toddler, Dan's
mother, when discussing her other grandchildren,
stated right in front of Kayla: "We love Kayla but
Breana and Brady are blood." At one point she called
me while Dan was at work and spoke harshly to me,

so much so that I began to hyperventilate, something I had never done before.

With multiple stress factors, I sunk further into depression and began to have many sleepless nights. I began taking prescription drugs to ease the depression and help me get the rest I needed. Meanwhile, while all this was happening, we put on a smiling face and faithfully attended and participated in church services.

CHAPTER SIX

The Scarlet Letter D

One warm Sunday morning in the spring, our family attended church. After the service in the worship center, the kids headed to their classes and Dan and I went to the "Marriage by Design" class. The class was set up with round tables, seating up to eight people around each one. We had been to it before, but we weren't regulars. We sat at a table with a young couple I knew; they were the "table leaders" for the discussions. I don't remember the topic, but I remember the question that was posed directly to us as a couple. Because the young man knew I had been heavily involved in ministry and had been on staff there previously, he thought we would be a perfect couple to ask. "With your involvement in the ministry and the stress that it can bring, how do you and Dan keep your marriage alive and growing? What are the things you do to make it work?"

After we both stammered…uh…uh.., I opened my mouth and said, "Well, we pray together and read the Bible together…." I tried to pull out anything that would sound good. After all, I had been in church all my life and I knew what I had to say to look good. As I was speaking, I had the strange experience of seeing myself talking to everyone, looking in from the outside. I watched myself lie! Lying in church to everyone at the table. After the yuck flowed from my lips, my face felt flushed, and I couldn't wait to get the class over with.

I remember walking down the church hallway as we were leaving, Dan and the children a few steps ahead. In a deep conversation with myself, I said, "I'm damned if I do; I'm damned if I don't. Either way I am sinning. If I stay in the marriage, I'm lying and living a lie to everyone around me. If I leave, I am sinning by getting a divorce. Damned if I do, damned if I don't. What's the worst of the two evils? I feel trapped."

Lunch was quiet that day. We methodically got through the meal with the kids, sent them on their way to play or do their own thing, and then cleaned up the kitchen. I headed to the bedroom where I had been sleeping alone. I thought about the repercussions of a divorce. I thought about what my parents' reactions would be and what my friends would think of me. I knew that possibly I would no longer be a part of the church I was attending. As I pondered over what everyone else would think of me and my situation, I realized I was doing what I had always done. I was worrying about what everyone else thought and how I could live my life to please others. Why was I always trying to appear as something I was not?

Then it came to me: This is my life, not someone else's life. It is mine to live, and no one can live it for me. They are not in my shoes. I have to live my life for me, not how others think I should live it." Then I asked myself a very difficult question: "Am I willing to lose my parents and my friends with the decision I am about to make? If I do this, am I ready to be alone without any support?" I don't know how I came to the conclusion that "Yes, I am willing and ready to let it go," but I did. My resolve was strong. Of course, I was very concerned about the children, about how they would react and handle the news, especially with all the other chaotic things happening in our lives. Yet I was unequivocally ready.

Soon I called Dan to the room and asked him to sit down. "I have to talk to you and we have to be honest. Dan, how long has it been since we've slept together in the same bed?"

Dan said, "Seven years."

I shook my head, "There is nothing there. There never has been anything there. I knew when I walked down the aisle. You've known all these years."

Dan nodded in agreement. "Yes, I know."

Amicably, we discussed what we would do. We offered support to one another and decided we would begin the separation and divorce proceedings. We agreed to sell our house, move into separate homes, share joint custody with the children, and do our best to make a difficult situation as easy as possible for everyone, especially the children. Dan and I kept our friendship and wished each other the best for the future.

The first night that we were separated, I slept like a baby. I didn't notice that I had left my depression medication and sleeping pills behind until the next evening. It was too late to get them, so I decided to try to sleep again that night without them. Again, I slept like a baby. From that day forward, I never took another pill for depression or sleeplessness!

The hardest part about going through a divorce is telling family and friends. I waited as long as I could so that Dan and I could settle ourselves before bringing in the disruption of others' opinions. I had already disappointed my family enough. I remembered how my father took it when I told him I was pregnant with Kayla, and I knew this would not sit well with him at all. Though there were divorces in the extended family, there were none in the immediate family. I would be the first and only one in our family to get a divorce. I couldn't bring myself to tell anyone, so I wrote a letter. As expected, the response came in the form of my wedding invitation with Scripture verses all over it and asking me if the devil had gotten a hold of me. My impending divorce was big news and a shock to my family. Every one of them lived at least 10 hours away, so they didn't know much about anything that had been going on. After all, we had hidden it from the church that was less than 15 minutes away for years!

I understood where my father was coming from. I was not raised to believe that divorce is acceptable in any way, shape or form. I still don't believe in divorce and would counsel anyone to stay married. I believe in "What God has joined together, let no man put asunder." But I didn't believe this marriage was put together by God. I was obviously warned three times before I got married not to do it. But then I would tell myself that I was just rationalizing; I hated it when others would rationalize; I didn't want to be like that. I believe divorce is a sin like any other. But it is not the unpardonable sin. I believe Jesus' words concerning divorce and adultery (Matthew 5:31, 32). I know that Scripture also says if a Christian has a spouse "who isn't a believer [and] insists on leaving, let them go. In such cases, the husband or wife is no longer bound to the other, for God has called you to live in peace." (I Corinthians 7:15) Though that wasn't the exact reason in our case, I also know that God is a God of peace and order. I tried my best to do what was right and stayed in the marriage for 15 years because I didn't *believe* in divorce. So I understood how my family felt, but it didn't stop my spirit from hurting. I did receive some support from my brother and was thankful to have one family member I knew I could count on.

The next person on my list to tell was my friend Mary. Mary and I had met working at the headquarters of a prominent church denomination, and she and her husband were also involved in ministry outside of the church. I wasn't sure how she would take my news and if she would fall into line with the religious criticism and no longer be a part of my life. I had prepared myself for the worst when I met her one Saturday morning for coffee. At first we made the usual small talk before we got down to the personal, as we had many times before when we met for breakfast. As the conversation got deeper, my heart started pounding.

"Mary I have something to tell you and it's big," I said. "This is hard."

"Come on, Angie. You know you can tell me. What do you think—that I'm going to judge you?"

"Dan and I are getting a divorce."

Mary's comeback was astonishing. "I'm not surprised."

"What?" I exclaimed.

"You didn't think I knew? Angela, I could tell by the look in your eyes that there was nothing there," she said assuredly.

I was relieved and astounded at the same time. If she saw it, how many others knew? Mary gave me her full support and told me she would be there if I needed to talk to anyone. Every day, I was beginning to feel a little lighter with the load I had been carrying. The word was out and I had a brother and a friend who were there for me. I knew the rest of the world might place the big scarlet letter "D" across my forehead and condemn me to die. But I only had to answer to One Judge and to myself for the trajectory of my life.

CHAPTER SEVEN

The Aftermath

Within less than two months of the conversation with Dan that Sunday morning, we were divorced. Everything was agreed upon and carried out without any problems whatsoever. Surprisingly, my daughter took it the hardest. My son seemed to handle the changes fairly well. Only time would tell how this would affect them. Dan and I tried to keep the communication lines open between us and the children.

At times, Seth would get tired of me asking how he was doing, what he thought, and if he was okay. But his grades continued to be at the top and there weren't any behavioral changes. He was adjusting well.

As for Kayla, her behavior continued as it was before. I knew I would not be able to deal effectively with her alone, so she lived with Dan who did his best to work with her. Eventually her behavior escalated with him to the point that he called me crying over an incident that had just happened. He had tried to enforce the punishment of grounding and she walked out the door anyway. He had followed her out the door to try to get her to come back in. Instead she ran cussing him out in front of the neighbors. He said he had never been so humiliated in his life. It was the ultimate for him and I had not heard Dan like this before. That was enough for me and we both decided to make good on a threat and send her to her biological father — Nick.

Kayla had met Nick and his family when she was seven years old and one other time for Nick's mother's 80th birthday party. She had occasionally spoken with him on the phone over the years…more so as she got older. Sometimes she would use her relationship with Nick, as little as it was, against Dan, saying that her real Dad understood her better. But Nick was nowhere near his family in Missouri at that time. He was living near the Mexican border in New Mexico. We knew this would be a rough move, but maybe there was something more that Nick could do for her that we couldn't. Maybe she would go there and appreciate her family here more. We spoke with Nick on the phone and he was in full agreement. Within a few days, Dan had her get her traveling bags ready, as well as boxes full of items that would be sent to her after her arrival. I ordered the plane tickets and Dan took her to the airport. I couldn't even bare to go there to say good-bye one more time, out of fear that I would change my mind when I saw her. It was typical we would get suckered in by her pleadings, only to experience the same behavior time and time again.

After only two weeks of her being there, Nick called and said, "The honeymoon is over." I told him I was not surprised. She was disobeying him, staying out all night, and they were ultimately getting in fights with her taking swings at him. He hung in there and enrolled her in school. She stayed with him for nearly nine months until a phone conversation between Nick and I erupted and he decided to send her back to me. He was going to send my 16-year-old daughter home on an overnight bus trip from near the Mexican border, where he was living, to Missouri. He was doing this to save money and seemed to have no concern for her safety. Of course, I wasn't going to have that, and I had him book her a flight.

I spoke with Kayla about doing simple chores

and following the house rules concerning curfew, and about helping her to get her driver's license. She had not passed her driver's test yet and needed support and driving practice. Kayla agreed and soon she was back in my home.

I was nervous about how we would get along. At first, all was going well but after a few weeks, she began "doing her own thing" again. She broke her curfew, neglected to do her chores, and began cursing and doing whatever she wanted. Though I helped her get her license and bought her a car, she showed only disrespect and no appreciation. Over the next few months before her 17th birthday, things were even worse than before. It seemed no matter what I did, she responded with anger.

There comes a point that you realize that you have done all you can, when you are at your breaking point, and that ultimately the other person has to take responsibility. Sometimes love has to be tough and you have to let someone go, so that God can deal with them.

We let her go out on her own at age 17. It was an excruciating decision. There were times where we didn't know if she would finish school. After talking to the school counselor, I gave Kayla a call and encouraged her to not give up so close to receiving her diploma. Thankfully, Kayla completed high school. On her graduation night, Dan and I were filled with great joy and relief. Dan, Seth and I were there together cheering loudly as she made her way across the stage to receive her diploma.

CHAPTER EIGHT

MO No More

The past few years have been a search for, and a discovery of, who I am and what I should be doing with my life. That kind of trip is not an easy one. Often it is full of steep hills and turns and near fatal crashes.

I became successful in real estate in Missouri, purchased a home, and lived comfortably as the market and referrals flowed to me. I was settled physically but unsettled spiritually. I had searched for happiness out in the world but quickly came back to my spiritual roots. I became involved at a church in a nearby town and joined the choir. A year went by virtually uneventfully, but then something strange began to happen.

I would regularly see license plates from California, and when I was driving down the highway there was a particular song that would play on the radio, one I hadn't heard for a long time, but it had always reminded me of California. Now to most people that would be no big deal, but to me this meant something. While I was married, we had visited California and for some reason I had a strong desire to move to California at that time, but I didn't understand why. Dan even looked into transferring our family there, but we couldn't justify the cost with what Dan's company was going to pay him, so those plans were put off. I still had in my heart a desire to live in that state. You could've asked me any day what state I would be willing to move to and I would've said California. As crazy as it sounded, and with all the negatives I heard about the state, along with hearing about people moving to Missouri from California, I continued to have this little warm tug at my heart. So every time I saw a license plate, my heart skipped a beat.

I didn't dwell on the thought of moving there, but prayed for God to use me and do something with my life. I would hear of God calling other people in the church to other states and I wanted God to call me.

One Sunday morning, my son and I attended worship services. I was on the platform with the choir when I became still before the Lord as I looked over the congregation. I had that same Voice I had heard before in my spirit say, "This is no longer your church family. I have a new place for you." Tears welled up in my eyes. I sat with my son listening to the sermon while beginning to feel a peaceful disconnection. Afterwards, my son walked out to the foyer as I spoke to one of the godly women in the church. I told her what I had experienced in my heart and she prayed for me that God would clarify and give me direction. When my son and I got back to the car, he asked me why I was crying. I told him that I felt God was calling me to California and I didn't want to leave him and didn't really know when this would happen.

His response was impeccable. "Mom, if God wants you to go to California, then go. I will stay with dad and I will be fine. Besides, when I come out there to visit, I can play golf on some of the finest golf courses." I cried and hugged him. I told him I loved him, as I did on a daily basis.

I didn't have a clue as to when everything would take place. It could be months. It could be years. I took out an online study to prepare for getting a real estate license in California. Many times I would let the study sit and not do anything, but I knew I was running out of time to complete it. If the time expired, I would have to pay for the course all over again and that was something I was unwilling to do. So I pulled myself together and focused on completing the course. By October 2006, I had completed the course, flown out to San Diego and passed my real estate license exam. While visiting there I met with a couple of real estate brokers in Southern California. I knew when I looked at the map that I would end up somewhere between L.A. and San Diego, along the coast to within an hour or so inland, but I had no clarity until I asked one of the brokers when I got back home. He told me that after meeting me he felt that Monarch Beach or Mission Viejo would be a good fit for me.

I began researching and found out more about Mission Viejo. I had visited there once before and knew that it wasn't far from Saddleback Church. This church had been recommended to me and I had visited there a couple of times on previous visits. In February 2007, my real estate license was formally issued from the state of California. Even with the license in hand and direction to a specific location, I still did not know the timing. All I knew was that my license was good for four years so I had plenty of time. Maybe I would wait until Seth graduated. I was never one to rush into anything and would check out the situation from different angles before making any move. Sometimes even with all the facts, God had to push me through the door.

After working out at the gym one evening, I had plans to go to the store with my son. Usually I like to get cleaned up after a workout but for some strange reason I felt an urgency to pick up Seth as stinky as I was and go straight to the store. When we arrived at the store, I found a spot on the next aisle of cars and pulled in. Immediately, I saw it. "Oh brother!" My son barely said the word "what?" when he saw it too. The car parked in front of us had California license plates. My son knew what had been going on. We laughed at seeing another plate and I breathed words to the Lord: "Okay...it's one thing to see the license plates. It would be something if the person actually came to that car and I could talk to them." At that moment, the lady came to the car and began unlocking her door. I fumbled with my door, trying to open it quickly. I made my way to her and we began talking. She had moved to Missouri not far from me, and before that, had lived in Los Angeles for years. She told me about her church, and, ironically, the name of her church in California was the same name as mine in Missouri—Hope Community! We exchanged contact information and she also gave me the name of a friend of hers who was a real estate agent there. She told me to contact her if I had any questions whatsoever.

Soon after that I was talking to a friend and I told her about what had just happened. She exclaimed, "What more do you need to tell you that you are supposed to move to California — a billboard!?"

I worked hard in real estate, not knowing when I'd actually be moving. After all, I needed money to move out there. Just as my career was beginning to soar, I was sensing that it was time. All my agent friends thought I was crazy. "Angela, you are at the top of your game. Things are starting to happen for you." They were right, but my take was that God was providing the income so I could go.

Rapidly, all the questions I had were answered in a short amount of time. I knew where I was moving to, where I would live, what church I would attend, and who would be renting the home I was in. With the moving truck rented, and fellow agents helping me to load up, I was on the road and in California the first Saturday of June 2007. Before I left, I had ten listings and I sold all but one. Four of my closings actually came after I moved to California.

I didn't know what to think of my move. It was a new experience; feelings that I had never had before.

I had never done this big a move outside of going to college when I was 18. But this was completely different. Though my daughter was out on her own and my son was a sophomore in High School, I could hardly bare the thought of leaving them. Especially since my son was not on his own yet. I struggled with this many times over the next year and a half. Then on January 5, 2009, I was alone with God and cried out to him about my feelings, asking many questions, including whether I should return to Missouri. I received very clear answers:

1. That God was teaching my son character building skills, and that I wasn't to go back to "rescue him" because then the opportunity for him to learn those things would diminish.
2. That I would be together with my son again.
3. That I was not to look back like Lot's wife but to move forward.

By the time I was finished seeking the answers, I had nine pages in my journal full of direction and Scriptures to lead the way. Not only that, I had peace in my heart to move forward.

The following summer my son and I visited colleges in Central and Southern California. Divine direction was leading the way and my son had found one that he wanted to go to just four hours away from where I lived. Had I not lived here, I don't know that he would have even thought to come out here. Seth said to me, "Mom, maybe you came out here for me."

In October he applied and in December he received confirmation of his acceptance. What is amazing is that we were informed at the college day assembly that there were 8000 applicants for fall 2010 and less than 1100 applicants were accepted! I had also heard that he was in the first round of acceptance because I was a resident of California. And because of having joint custody and my claiming him on taxes, he would get in-state tuition. The Bible says, "The steps of a righteous man are ordered of the Lord." The Lord definitely ordered these steps to prepare for my son's future.

I have seen God work in other ways since I have been in California. Though some days have not been easy, rest assured I have followed the rough path to do what was asked of me. The day after I moved here, I joined Saddleback Church in Lake Forest and within months joined the Praise Choir. Whether being involved at the church in the choir, ensemble, singing a solo, or speaking somewhere, I have grown in ways that I would have never imagined. The friendships I've cultivated have blessed me beyond my imaginings, and God has used me to make a difference in other people's lives including leading someone to the Lord. Being here wasn't only about me, but about far reaching plans for others. Every decision we make affects those around us—some more than we will ever know.

Epilogue

I vividly remember sitting in the car in front of the abortion clinic when I found out I was pregnant. I'm happy to say that the clinic is now a Christian owned adoption and foster care ministry.

My family is my biggest supporters, especially my parents, who have been married for 61 years now. My dad has turned into an 80 year old salesman sharing my book to family, friends, and even a couple of bookstores!

Kayla is now married to Michael, who is in the army and has served in Afghanistan, and they have a son, David — my first grandchild. My beautiful daughter is a strong and determined woman and I believe that God has special plans for her in this world.

As for my son Seth, he continued on a steady path and graduated high school *summa cum laude* and will be attending a prestigious engineering school this fall within hours from where I live. God has always had his hand on his life and I am looking forward to seeing God's plan unfold with him.

Dan, five years after the divorce, is now married. I expressed how happy I was for him and wished him and his wife the very best. He then told me that he hoped that I would find someone too someday. We both truly want the best for each other in life and love. Dan is a good man and he deserves love and happiness.

As for me, I am single and doing my best to listen to God's voice in my life. The pain of this story is over and healing has come. I realize that the afflictions we go through work in us to mold us into who we are to become. Through this I have learned that God is not punishing, but He is shaping. And when you let go of all you thought you should have been and open yourself up to what God has for you, you'll become what He has planned all along.

"Yet God has made everything beautiful for its own time." (Ecclesiastes 3:11)

Part II

CHAPTER NINE

Thoughts for Singles

My prayer is that you will learn from my failures and strive to live a life pleasing to the Lord. With all the opportunities to follow what the world would have you believe and do, even Christians are lulled into accepting things that are clearly against God's best plan and purpose for their lives today. I have been told by Christians that they believe it is okay to have sex even though they are not married, as long as they are only having sex with the person they are in a relationship with. Is it any wonder why singles are staying single longer? They have everything they want until they are ready to move on to the next person. There is no commitment. One pastor proclaimed from the pulpit, "I have never seen a more non-committal generation in all my life. No one wants to commit because they are afraid something better might come along." God's Word is still unchanging, despite what we think or feel. I Corinthians 6:9-20 (NLT) says:

> *"Don't you realize that those who do wrong will not inherit the Kingdom of God? Don't fool yourselves. Those who indulge in sexual sin, or who worship idols, or commit adultery, or are male prostitutes, or practice homosexuality, or are thieves, or greedy people, or drunkards, or abusive, or cheat people - none of these will inherit the Kingdom of God. Some of you were once like that. But you were cleansed; you were made holy; you were made right with God by calling on the name of the Lord Jesus Christ and by the Spirit of our God.*
>
> *You say, "I am allowed to do anything." But not everything is good for you. And even though you are allowed to do anything, you must not become a slave to anything. You say, "Food was made for the stomach, and the stomach for food." (This is true, though someday God will do away with both of them.) But you can't say that our bodies were made for sexual immorality. They were made for the Lord, and*

the Lord cares about our bodies. And God will raise us from the dead by his power, just as he raised our Lord from the dead.

Don't you realize that your bodies are actually parts of Christ? Should a man take his body, which is a part of Christ, and join it to a prostitute? Never! And don't you realize that if a man joins himself to a prostitute, he becomes one body with her? For the Scriptures say, "The two are united into one." But the person who is joined to the Lord is one spirit with him.

Run from sexual sin! No other sin so clearly affects the body as this one does. For sexual immorality is a sin against your own body. Don't you realize that your body is the temple of the Holy Spirit, who lives in you and was given to you by God? You do not belong to yourself, for God bought you with a high price. So you must honor God with your body."

Are there any "buts" to what the Word says? I don't know of any. Regardless of what my opinion is or what I am feeling, there is no watering down of the clarity of the Scriptures. I would be the last one to preach regarding this, for who am I? I can only deliver the message.

Curiosity, peer pressure and compromising circumstances can lead you down a path that will forever change the course of your life. This change can be through an unwanted pregnancy, numerous venereal diseases, AIDS, or emotional memories and physical ties, as well as the degrading and depriving of yourself by giving your precious body to someone other than the person you marry.

God, the Father, doesn't give us commands just to stifle our fun. Jesus said that He came so that you might have life more abundantly (John 10:10). He made sex for the husband and wife to become one with each other and to enjoy the fullest intimacy that only belongs to those who are married. He is not taking anything away. Instead He has guidelines to provide for us and to protect us. Think about it! He loves us so much that He wants to protect us from all the mental and physical hang-ups, so He can provide a fulfilling sex life in the confines of marriage. The God who made you, who gave His Son to die for you does not give you commands to spoil your fun. I only wished I had understood this deep in my spirit when I was younger.

When you give up your body to someone, you are giving up more than your virginity or just having sex. A part of your emotions and spirit goes with that person because you have become one. What is sad is that, when you are in another relationship, inevitably there is the discussion of the previous relationships and what you did with that other person. Instead of innocence, there is comparison. I have known only two couples in my life that have kept themselves accountable and pure until their wedding day. Can you imagine the precious gift they gave to each other? They gave every part of their being, not just their bodies.

It's easy to let feelings and emotions lead you to passionate regret. Joseph, when he was tempted by the Pharaoh's wife, didn't allow himself to think "Hmm, she looks so good," or "I could probably get away with this." Genesis 39:10-12 says that Joseph *"kept out of her way as much as possible."* And later when she grabbed him and begged him to have sex with her, Joseph *"tore himself away"* and RAN! Get the thought in your mind beforehand. RUN! I know it's not easy. You have to settle it in your mind and your character long before you are tempted. You have to know who you are and what you will do to protect your character.

If you think you have found the "one" that you are going to spend your life with then you can wait a little longer. Protect the one you love. Relationships fail and new ones begin. Feelings are nothing but emotional roller coasters. You'll feel "this is the one" more than once because the devil will make sure of that. If it's right, then wait. When you honor God in your singleness, He'll bless you in your marriage.

To those who's temptation is toward sexual sin and you have fallen, Jesus will forgive you, if you ask. *"He is faithful and just to forgive you of your sin and to cleanse you from all unrighteousness"* (I John 1:9). If you have consequences like I did, confide in someone. Don't get an abortion. That child was "knitted in the womb" by God himself. He knows every intricate detail of who that child will be. If you decide that you cannot raise the child, there is already a family that God has in mind to "bring that child up in the way that he should go." God is well acquainted with your ways and He knows what you need. If you are the one who fathered a child, take responsibility; offer support, and help with the decisions as to the future of this precious little one.

If you have not suffered any obvious consequences, you need to humbly thank God that He had mercy and you have come to your senses in time to get a handle on your life. But do not take the grace of God for granted. *"Well then, should we keep on sinning so that God can show us more and more of his wonderful grace? Of course not! Since we have died to sin, how can we continue to live in it?"* (Galatians 6:1-2) In Galatians 2:21, Paul says, *"I do not treat the grace of God as meaningless."*

For some, the task of purity is not an easy one. Each person has their own temptations and struggles. We must remember that we cannot do this by ourselves. We need God, close Christian friends, and godly counsel to walk with us as we tread this journey we are on. Put God first in everything you do and watch Him paint the picture of your life into something more beautiful than you could ever imagine. *"Now unto Him who is able to do exceedingly, abundantly above all that we could ask or think"* (Ephesians 3:30), and to Him who *"is able to keep you from falling and to present you faultless before the presence of his glory with exceeding joy"* (Jude v. 24 & 25).

CHAPTER TEN

Thoughts for Parents

The challenges faced by parents today are astronomical. As a parent who has raised two teenagers, I understand the challenges, disappointments, hopes, dreams, and successes of parenthood. I have been on both sides of the fence—on one side as a wayward young lady; on the other, as a parent with great pain and great joy.

Basic biblical principles tell us how to raise our children. We are told that children are a blessing of the Lord (Psalm127:3) and that we are to *"teach them in the morning and night"* (Deut. 6:1-9). We are to raise our children in the *"admonition of the Lord"* and not to *"provoke our children to anger"* (Eph. 6:4). But many times we fall short of doing our best as a parent. Just one wrong action can have an impact that not only affects the future but affects someone's eternity. I am definitely not a model parent, even though I love my children more than they'll ever know. And though I didn't always understand the discipline I received as a child, I understand the love of a parent who wants their children to do what is right.

Even Jesus' anger burned over the money changers at the temple so much so He threw over the tables! (John 2:15) But that anger was from a burning love that wanted purity in His house. And as a parent, when we see our children go astray, our love for them, and anger for the sin, sometimes gets misconstrued as lack of love for them. Many times we simply don't know how to discipline our children, and what may work for one, may not work for the other one.

Though every situation is different, with anyone, the best you can do is to keep the lines of communication open. Tell them of the many consequences of disobeying God's Word and the blessing God brings when we follow His plan and come under His protection and provision. And listen, listen, listen. That is something I wish I would've done more of. We get so busy doing our jobs, trying to pay the bills, and volunteering at the church (many times way too much), that we don't spend real time with our children. I know with my daughter, we had to sometimes sit and wait awhile before what was in her heart came out. That takes patience!

After you've established this open relationship, then you pray. Pray with them. I routinely every night would tuck my children in, even when they were teenagers, and pray for them. Occasionally, I would pray for them at other times, but regrettably, not nearly as much as I should have. Praying should not be something that we do only over a meal or before bedtime. Children must see the battles we fight in the spirit on a consistent basis. They must hear you when you are crying out to God in the rough times, and they must hear you give praise to Him for every blessing.

One thing that has troubled me is that I was the one who had the task of leading them spiritually. I wanted their father to also show leadership in this area, but he never did. Men, fathers, please don't let your spouse or your children's mother exclusively take the lead. Your children need your leadership too. You are the head under Christ. Many men take the back seat when it comes to leading their families spiritually and emotionally. I guarantee that if more fathers were present in their daughters' lives, showing them how they are to be treated, more girls would have the confidence they need to earn the respect they deserve. And your sons will watch you and see how you treat their mother and sister and follow your path. This is so important for our children. We have long glossed over a man's role, allowing the women's movement to undermine the man's role in the family and turn him into a weak role model. My hope is that men will find out once again who they are in Christ so that they can be better parents for future generations.

Yet there are times that even when we've done all that we can do, we are told to *"stand firm"* (Eph. 6:13, 14). Moses said in the battle against the Egyptians, *"Fear not, stand still and see the salvation of the Lord"* (Ex. 14:13). When you feel inadequate as a parent and feel you've messed up, you must trust in the grace and mercy of God. And if you are one of those parents who truly believe you did all you could, and still your child has gone astray farther than you could have imagined, then all you can do is trust God to bring your child back. Either way, whether or not you have regrets in your parenting, the bottom line is that when they are grown they are in God's hands completely. They are not in your control anymore. Parents, you cannot control or change your children's negative and destructive behaviors when they are grown. Let them go! Give them 100% to the Lord. Who better to give them to?

You can trust the One who created them. He knows when they sit down, when they stand up, and every thought they have. He knows and is familiar with _all_ their ways! (Psalm 139:2)

When you've given them sincerely to the Lord from your heart, and you pray for them, you will know how you need to respond. No matter what the situation, whether it's pregnancy, drugs, alcohol or any other problem, God will give you wisdom (James 2) when you ask Him.

Though circumstances and situations may vary, I know from my experience that forgiveness and strong support would have made all the difference. There is no need to be preachy with your child at this time, especially if they've been in church at all, because they will know. And the last thing you want to do is criticize them when they are down. That would be like giving someone a few hard kicks when they are writhing on the floor in pain. Ask yourself: What is the loving response? How would I want to be responded to if it were me? Would I be ashamed of my response before God, the church or friends? If it wasn't for God's grace, where would I be?

When we put the situation in perspective from the other person's point of view, and when we can take a detached view (as a third party viewing the scene), we can gather the information needed to form the appropriate response with grace. Our children deserve the same hand of forgiveness that you would offer to your closest friends. Many times we are harsh in our response to the ones nearest to us — our family. But Ephesians 4:32 says, *"Instead, be kind to each other, tenderhearted, forgiving one another, just as God through Christ has forgiven you."* Not only the Scriptures that talk about children, but all the other Scriptures that talk about love and compassion also apply to our children. We cannot differentiate in our treatment of family and friends! The same rules apply, and we sometimes forget that when we relate to family members.

There is nothing better than getting direct instruction from the Lord. Who better knows your situation? Who knows your children's hearts better? Who has perfect wisdom to lead you in the correct path? Seek the Lord, pray with and for your children, communicate deeply, love deeply, forgive deeply, and be fiercely compassionate.

May God bless you in your endeavors to guide and direct your children, so that *"all your children will be taught of the Lord and great will be the peace of your children"* (Isaiah 43:9).

CHAPTER ELEVEN

Thoughts for the Church

First of all, I want to thank and show respect to those God has called into full-time ministry. The responsibility and burden of leading others in service to Christ is great, yet its rewards are unmatched. Second, I am grateful for the many in the church that are living God's grace and mercy in reaching to others in compassion. There is now more help and support, and more programs that are helping young people in their commitment to purity and helping divorcees to recover from their loss. Much has been done and more can be done with the correct attitudes.

Though a great number of the members of various churches have *head* knowledge concerning the Scriptures, many more do not have *heart* knowledge. Church members who take a Pharisaical approach to those who have fallen, that is, with their nose up in the air and pointing a condemning finger, do even more harm by causing the condemned person to go even further away from God's truth, and causing them to make more bad decisions in their lives. How many of these unfortunates, after being so cruelly treated, have left the church, never to return? How many have allowed what the church says about what they can or cannot do dictate a future that does not serve them well?

Thankfully, I am currently a part of a church that not only preaches but lives what it preaches. From the pulpit on down, there is love, acceptance and forgiveness. The members of the church demonstrate God's love and compassion and consequently many lives have been changed. I have seen single, pregnant women stand before the church and get a loving standing ovation followed by love and personal care. I have seen drug addicts, sex addicts, people with low self-esteem, and people experiencing many other issues come to Christ and receive forgiveness, healing and deliverance by the church body being who they should be.

In a familiar story, John 8:1-11, a woman caught in the act of adultery was brought to Jesus. Her accusers wanted to stone her and try to trap Jesus into saying something they could use against Him. Jesus didn't rush to judgment. He knew the Scriptures more than anyone for He is the Word Himself. Deuteronomy 22:22 did say that both the man and woman must die if they commit adultery. Jesus didn't ask for them to bring the man and stone both of them, though He could have. Instead, thoughtfully and confidently, he responded, *"All right, but let the one who has never sinned throw the first stone!"*

Wow, they were not expecting Jesus to reply this way. What could they say? They were speechless! *"They slipped away one by one, beginning with the oldest, until only Jesus was left in the middle of the crowd with the woman."* Can you picture this in your mind? Now here is this woman who was caught in the midst of sin, dragged out to die before a crowd, and within a few minutes Jesus had spoken one sentence that gave her the opportunity to live! Alone with Jesus, while the crowd watched from a distance, Jesus asked her, *"Where are your accusers? Didn't even one of them condemn you?"* *"No, Lord,"* she said. And Jesus said, *"Neither do I. Go and sin no more."*

That's it????!!! No penalty? You mean she didn't have to pay time? She didn't have to do a service to make up for what she had done? No! Absolutely nothing! That is simply the grace of God. All of us have sinned. It only takes one sin to be considered a lawbreaker. Ecclesiastes 7:20 says, *"There is not a single person in all the earth who is always good and never sins."* Because we have sinned, no matter what the sin is, no matter how small we think it may seem, we do not have the right to judge someone on anything!

What should our response be? Galatians 6:1-3 has a clear message about what we should do. *"Dear brothers and sisters, if another <u>believer</u> is overcome by some sin, you who are godly should gently and humbly help that person back onto the right path. And be careful not to fall into the same temptation yourself. Share each other's burdens, and in this way obey the law of Christ. If you think you are too important to help someone, you are only fooling yourself. You are not that important."*

Vine's Expository Dictionary of New Testament Words talks about being "overtaken" and about "restoration." It says that "overtaken is not that of detecting a person in the act, but of his being caught by the trespass, through his being off his guard." And the word "restore" comes from the Greek word KATARTIZO which means "to mend, to furnish completely." It speaks of the "restoration, by those who are spiritual, of one overtaken in a trespass, such a one being a dislocated member of the spiritual body." Vine's goes on to say that the tense of the word "restore" is in the continuous present, suggesting the necessity for patience and perseverance in the process. Therefore, the church body is to set this Christian brother or sister back into place, like you would a dislocated bone, and surround him or her with support and stability, like a cast would do, until they are completely restored and able to function again properly in the body.

The "burden" in verse two is the Greek word BAROS which means "a heavy weight, a crushing load which will overwhelm a man unless he is given assistance" (*The Galatians: The Charter of Christian Liberty* by Merrill C. Tenney). I received burden lifting when Pastor Mike prayed and broke all condemnation. That was the beginning of my healing. The restoration process had also begun with the initial physical and financial support to get me started to prepare for my baby's arrival.

Where I believe many fail is that they stop short of completing the restoration process. It's like the person is set back into place (re-established), but the supporting cast is never put in place to help protect and strengthen them while they are in the healing process. So the person is always walking around *almost* whole but not completely healed. Many crucial life-changing decisions are still being made months and maybe even a year or years after getting re-established. The bigger the failure, the longer the restoration will be. You don't leave an alcoholic alone with a refrigerator full of beer after he's been free of use for a month. Neither do you pray for and give a little initial help to someone in need and say "good luck in your life, we've done our part," and send them on their way.

James 2:15-16 says, *"Suppose you see a brother or sister who has no food or clothing, and you say, 'Good-bye and have a good day; stay warm and eat well, but then you don't give that person any food or clothing. What good does that do?"* The basic principle of this verse is that when you see a need, don't just say kind words and be on your way. Fulfill the need! Through my struggles, I needed friendship and counsel. I know I would have benefitted greatly had someone come along and established a relationship with me and counseled me in my decisions in the year that followed. No doubt my life would have had a totally different outcome. At the same time, I am grateful for my two beautiful children and the struggles that have brought me to where I am today.

The God who was merciful enough to forgive David the adulterer and murderer, Moses the murderer, Rahab the harlot, the thief on the cross, and our own sin of pride and selfishness is the same God who can work miracles in each of our lives to bring about the righteousness of God. We do this by doing what Jesus said in Luke 6:36. *"You must be compassionate, just as your Father is compassionate."* Compassion and restoration until completion!

CHAPTER TWELVE

Clay in the Potter's Hands

I have two framed pictures on my wall that show a potter's hands shaping so carefully the vessel he is making. Under one picture are the following words:

> *Just think, you're here not by chance, but by God's choosing.*
>
> *HIS HAND formed you and made you the person you are.*
>
> *He compares you to no one else. You are one of a kind.*
>
> *You lack nothing that HIS GRACE can't give you.*
>
> *He has allowed you to be here at this time in history to fulfill HIS SPECIAL PURPOSE for this generation.*
>
> *— Roy Lessin*

Below the other framed picture are two Scripture verses:

> *"Oh Lord, THOU ART THE POTTER and we are the clay, and the work of thy hand."*
> (ISAIAH 64:8 KJV)

> *"For I know the plans I have for you,"* says the Lord. *"PLANS FOR GOOD and not for evil, to give you a future and a hope."*
> (JEREMIAH 29:11 KJV)

Though I have read those two framed pictures many times, tears still come to my eyes. Those things that cause us pain—whether by our own sin or mistakes, or pain inflicted by others—are tools in the Potter's hands to shape us into a beautiful vessel that can be used to pour out support and blessings to others. The vessel that God has made you to be was never meant to be placed on a mantel just to look pretty or discarded because of its brokenness. Every one of us has something that we have gone through that we can share with others and perhaps change their lives.

And that is what I am hoping that my life, my brokenness, and my healing will do.

For booking information contact:

Angela Stout
AngelActOne Enterprises LLC
P.O. Box 80633
Rancho Santa Margarita, CA 92688
Email: Angela@AngelActOne.com
www.AngelActOne.com